S.H.A.P.E.

FINDING & FULFILLING YOUR UNIQUE
PURPOSE FOR LIFE

ERIK REES

ZONDERVAN®

GRAND RAPIDS, MICHIGAN 49530 USA

PurposeDriven®

ZONDERVAN.COM/
AUTHOR**TRACKER**

ZONDERVAN®

S.H.A.P.E.
Copyright © 2006 by Erik E. Rees

Requests for information should be addressed to:
Zondervan, *Grand Rapids, Michigan 49530*

ISBN-13: 978-0-310-27418-6 (softcover)
ISBN-10: 0-310-27418-4 (softcover)

Interior design by Beth Shagene

Printed in the United States of America

06 07 08 09 10 11 12 • 21 20 19 18 17 16 15 14 13 12 11 10 9 8 7 6 5 4 3 2 1

CONTENTS

Uncovering Your S.H.A.P.E.

Unlocking Your Life

Unleashing Your S.H.A.P.E. for Life

FOREWORD
BY RICK WARREN

God has given every creature he made a special area of expertise to fulfill its purpose. For instance, some animals run, others hop, some swim, others burrow, and some fly. Each has a particular role to play based on the way they were shaped by God.

This is equally true of you and every other human being. You were uniquely designed, wired, and "shaped" by God to do certain things. You are not an assembly-line product, mass produced without any thought. You are a custom-designed, one-of-a-kind, original masterpiece.

In my book, *The Purpose Driven® Life*, I introduced the concept of S.H.A.P.E., a simple acrostic I created more than twenty years ago to help people remember five factors God uses to prepare and equip us for our purpose in life. These five shaping tools are our **S**piritual gifts, **H**eart, **A**bilities, **P**ersonality, and **E**xperiences. You are shaped to serve God by serving others.

Now, in this wonderful, long-needed book by Erik Rees, we have a more thorough, in-depth explanation of the implications and applications of S.H.A.P.E. Erik has served at my side at Saddleback Church for ten years. As our pastor of ministry, his job is to help people in our church family discover their S.H.A.P.E., find their niche, and experience the joy of being what God created them to be. He is *passionate* about helping people unlock their God-given potential, and I can say without any reservation that Erik understands more about helping you discern and develop your S.H.A.P.E. than any other person on the planet. This book will undoubtedly become the standard text on this subject in many schools.

Before architects design any new building, they first ask, "What will be its purpose? How will it be used?" The intended function always determines the form of the building. Before God created you, he decided what role he wanted you to play on earth. He planned exactly how he wanted you to serve him, and then he shaped you for those tasks. You are the way you are because you were made for a specific contribution on earth.

God never wastes anything. He would not give you abilities, interests, talents, gifts, personality, and life experiences unless he intended to use them for his glory. By identifying and understanding these factors, you can discover God's will for your life. I can guarantee that you are going to benefit from this book in an incredible way.

With more than thirty million readers of *The Purpose Driven® Life*, we are now seeing a movement of *purpose driven people* around the world who are embracing and expressing their unique shape in serving God and mankind. I invite you to join us in this movement!

Read this book with a friend, then share it with other friends. Then let us know how *you* are using your S.H.A.P.E. We'd love to hear from you. Email your story to us at *shape@purposedriven.com*. I'm excited about how much you are going to grow!

ACKNOWLEDGMENTS

Although this page was one of the last written, the pages that follow would never have been written if not for the people mentioned here. I am truly humbled to be among you all.

To my heavenly Father, I'm desperate without you! O how weak I am without you, God. I thank you for allowing me the privilege to help your people embrace their uniqueness and grasp their ultimate purpose in life. May everyone who embraces what you have called me to write bring you glory with their lives on earth. The fact that you have allowed me to write for you is just one more evidence of your unmerited grace and goodness.

To Stacey, the love of my life, I say, "I love you!" I would not have been able to write this for God if you had not helped me find him when you did. I'm forever grateful for your constant love, forgiveness, and encouragement. Because of you, I'm a better man!

To Shaya, Jessica, and JT, I say, "I miss you!" You have been so patient with me as I did my best to balance the time spent writing this book and our "tickle time." May you always know and feel that you and Mom are my top priorities.

To Jeff, Joy, J., Cheri, Scott, Kasey, Jeff, and Rocio, I say, "Thank you!" You're the best small group ever. Your constant prayer, love, encouragement, counsel, and wisdom have helped make me the man I am today. I'm continually grateful for you.

To Mark, Peg, and Shelly, I am grateful for you. Your support, research, edits, and constant encouragement kept me writing when I felt like stopping. Thank you!

To my personal board of advisors, know that I'm better because of you. Thanks for your continued coaching and sharpening. There is no way I would be where I am today without your investment in me.

To my Saddleback Church family, I say, "You inspire me." You are the most humble, caring servants of God. It is such a privilege to serve God with you. May God continue to bless you as you persist in blessing his people in your generation.

To the countless men and women who share a similar passion of seeing people reach their full potential in Christ, I say to you, "Thanks for paving the way!" I fully accept the fact that I stand on your shoulders. Your writings and teachings have impacted and inspired me in so many ways. I especially want to acknowledge the writings of my senior pastor Rick Warren, my mentor Tom Paterson, and the outstanding work of John Ortberg, Os Guinness, and Arthur F. Miller. With honor and a grateful heart, I continue the work you began many years ago by sharing this message with the next generation.

A MESSAGE FROM THE AUTHOR
Getting the Most Out of Your Journey

I am delighted you are here. It is no accident! God is at work in your life, and there is something here he wants you to understand, something that will unlock your potential and unleash his power in you. The fact that you are reading this book tells me you are a learner, someone who wants to experience God's full potential. Perhaps you have realized that there must be more to life than you are experiencing. Perhaps you long to honor God with your life – to become the person he created you to be and to make the contribution he desires you to make.

In his bestselling book, *The Purpose Driven® Life*, Rick Warren showcases the five shared purposes of every Christian: worship, fellowship, discipleship, ministry, and evangelism. At the end of the book, Rick challenges his readers to consider a series of questions, one of which is "What will be the contribution of my life?" *S.H.A.P.E.* helps answer that all-important question.

While Rick focuses on the *shared* purposes of life, this book will focus on helping you start to find and fulfill God's *specific* purpose for your life – the one thing that truly unleashes your strengths and passions for his glory. Discovering your specific purpose in life opens up the wonderful opportunity to use what God has given you to serve others in your generation – to fulfill your ultimate purpose and live a significant life. As Rick says, "Service is the pathway to real significance. It is through ministry that we discover the meaning of our lives."

The Journey Ahead

The path toward significance is an incredible journey with God. Though the effort is tough, it will bring your life joy like never before and peace like nothing else.

Let God guide you up to your personal mountaintop. Rest in his arms and let him lift you high above the noise and stress of your life. Marvel at the amazing vista as he offers to help you discern who you are and how uniquely he has created you.

During this time of exile from the world's loud distractions, listen obediently as your Father asks you to empty the bag you gradually have been filling with worries and man-made longings. Let him relieve you of the pain and confusion that weighs you down and pulls you from him.

Let his love hold your hand. Follow his lead as he prompts you to seek the support of others who will also walk this journey with you. Before you've begun your descent, you will be en route to grasping your ultimate purpose for life. When God's desires align with your dreams, you discover the confidence to accept your specific kingdom assignment.

He will show you the steps to take as you start fulfilling your purpose for life, inspiring you to pursue not a career, but a calling. As you reach the bottom of the mountain you might even begin to see the faces of those you love and are meant to lead. With God's wisdom, you'll invest into each of them so they too can discover their purpose for life.

This journey with God leaves you energized and focused on finishing life faithful and fulfilled.

In fact, this journey you are about to embark on already has helped thousands, if not millions, of people all around the world discover their God-given special design and the specific difference God desires for them to make on earth for his glory.

Age, gender, occupation—it doesn't matter. I have seen moms find freedom to make a difference right within the home. I have seen pastors embrace their uniqueness and commit to helping others do the same. I have seen collegians maximize their courses, once they understood God's plan for them. I have seen CEOs and teachers gain a new passion for their gifts and an increased desire to show God's love to those they influence.

I've seen high school students gain permission to be who God has made them to be instead of what their friends and culture tell them to be. I have seen those in retirement find renewed purpose and vision for their life. The truth is, God made everyone and made everyone unique—and that includes you!

Consider Journeying with Someone

During my research for this book, I was reminded of the value of friendships. Over 90 percent of the people I interviewed pointed to *some one*—not just some principle—who played a vital role in helping them find and fulfill their specific purpose in life. I actually use a whole team of people to help keep me accountable to what God is calling me to do on his behalf.

If someone comes to mind whom you could invite to begin this life-changing journey with you, give them a call.

A Prayer for Your Journey

Holy Father, please show me just how special you have made me. Take me wherever you need to, so I can experience you like never before. Ignite my heart. Let it forever burn for the things you desire most—people. Align my dreams and desires with yours.

Lord, I long to be known as a difference-maker. Show me the way and your will, so I can follow. I fully acknowledge that I'm nothing without you. Please grant me continued grace, love, and wisdom as I walk this journey with you.

God, give me strength to face my fears along the way. Fill me with your love. Make my motives pure and honorable. Teach me the things I still need to learn so I can truly honor you with all of my life. Grant me faith like never before. Help me move away from my comforts and closer to your callings.

Father, help me find and fulfill the specific purpose in life you created me for so I can do your work in my generation for your glory. Amen.

Let the journey begin!

Uncovering Your S.H.A.P.E.

Chapter 1

MASTERPIECE

Only You Can Be You

For we are God's masterpiece.
He has created us anew in Christ Jesus,
so that we can do the good things
he planned for us long ago.
Ephesians 2:10 (NLT)

Instead of trying to reshape yourself to be like someone else,
you should celebrate the shape God has given you.
Rick Warren, *The Purpose Driven® Church*

You are a masterpiece.

During my freshman year of college, I took an art class – not because it was my major, but purely for the fun of it. (Well, to be honest, I took the class because of a cute girl who also had signed up for it!) One of our assignments was to study works on display at area art museums and galleries. So one day a classmate and I drove to an art show.

The director of the gallery was an interesting woman with a genuine enthusiasm for her job. When she introduced us to a local artist, I was struck by the deep passion he had for his work. He had complete confidence in his own ability. He spoke highly of his creations, pointing out that each was a custom-made original. I was amazed by his keen attention to detail. To an artist, each piece is unique, formed first within the artist's mind before it is actually produced. The artist thoroughly explores every inch of the creation before he calls it complete.

There is another Artist – a Grand Master – whose attention to detail and whose interest in his creation far outweigh that of any artist you will ever meet in a gallery. The Scripture says, "Thank you for making me so wonderfully complex! Your workmanship is marvelous – and how well I know it. You watched me as I was being formed in utter seclusion, as I was woven together in the dark of the womb. You saw me before I was born. Every day of my life was recorded in your book. Every moment was laid out before a single day had passed" (Psalm 139:14 – 16, NLT).

The Bible says you are the special creation of God Almighty, made in his own image so your life could make a significant difference for his kingdom. The God of the entire universe began making a masterpiece of you even as you were taking shape in your mother's womb. God himself is the one who breathed life into you.

God doesn't create anything without value. He is the ultimate craftsman. And he designed you specifically to fulfill a unique role in his ultimate plan to establish his kingdom on earth. Even though each of us has made mistakes that make it more difficult for him to perfect, we still are a special work of the Creator's hands. He even takes time to know about our day-to-day lives. In fact, he is smiling right now, rejoicing as you seek to discover the masterpiece you are to him.

The Bible says, "For we are God's masterpiece. He has created us anew in Christ Jesus, so that we can do the good things he planned for us long ago" (Ephesians 2:10, NLT).

This verse helps us understand that if we want to discover our mission or purpose in life, we first need to look at the masterpiece God has made us to be. While self-help books tell you to *look within*, I'm saying the key to living the life you were meant to live is to *look to God* and ask him to help you discover your uniqueness. Once you discover *who* you are, then you can start figuring out *what* God has planned for you, the specific way he designed you to make a difference in the world for him.

Another translation of Ephesians 2:10 uses the word *workmanship* to describe our uniqueness. It's from the Greek word *poiema*, which literally means "work of art," and is the root of our English word *poem*. You are a work of God—and nothing but the highest and best comes from his hand. Like the artist who takes scrap metal and turns it into an amazing sculpture, God takes our lives and fashions them into a masterpiece.

One of a Kind

You are not only a masterpiece shaped by God's own loving hands, but you are a unique work of divine art. Like an original painting or sculpture, you are a one of a kind. There is no one else like you, which is why your heavenly Father longs for you to discover just how special and unique you are. As Rick Warren says in *The Purpose Driven® Life*, "Only you can be you. God designed each of us so there would be no duplication in the world. No one has the exact same mix of factors that make you unique."

Perhaps that was one reason you picked up this book. You long to discover how special and unique you are. You're excited by the thought that God is creating a masterpiece of you, but you just don't see it in the reality of your life.

I want you to know, you are not alone in those feelings. As a pastor, I have worked with so many people who share the same longing. I have discovered that people truly *want* to be who God made them to be—and genuinely desire to do the work he is calling them to do. Most simply don't have the tools to get there.

The book you hold in your hand is designed to take you through a proven process, guided by the Holy Spirit, to discover who God created you uniquely to be—so you can start finding and fulfilling God's specific purpose for your life.

Our family has a Christmas tradition in which all the kids get to pick a favorite book for me to read to them. After I read what they have chosen, I read my choice—Max Lucado's engaging children's book, *You Are Special*. I love this book for many reasons, but especially because it reminds my children that they are unique in God's eyes.

Lucado tells the story of the Wemmicks, a community of painted wooden people. The conditions of their paint vary widely—from shiny and new to chipped and peeling. Each day, stickers are distributed in Wemmicksville. Some Wemmicks receive gold stars, while others are given gray dots.

One day, Punchinello, the main character, realizes that it's the pretty, shiny Wemmicks who get the stars, while those with tired, chipped paint receive the nondescript gray dots. He notices his own dots are all gray and concludes he must not be worth much, as Wemmicks go.

Then Punchinello meets Lucia, who wears neither stars nor dots. When she explains that the labels just never stick to her, Punchinello decides he wants to be "free" of stickers too. Lucia takes Punchinello to meet Eli, the creator of all Wemmicks, and Punchinello is amazed to learn that Eli loves him just the way he made him. Eli explains that the stickers only stick to those who allow them to remain stuck.

You Are Special is ripe with the meaning of unconditional love. Although intended for children, I'm encouraged by it myself. I appreciate how Eli, the loving woodcarver, took time to help Punchinello see just how special he was, regardless of what others thought or said about him. Like Punchinello, we all need to take time to visit with our Creator. How else can he demonstrate to us how we stand apart from all his other works of art?

God wants you to truly understand and accept who he has made you to be. He longs for you to experience the release that comes with simply living as the person he created you to be.

When it comes to being unique, I love how my mentor Tom Paterson describes it:

The fascinating thing to me is that literally everything God makes is unique—every human, animal, flower, tree, and every blade of grass. He didn't clone anything. Even identical twins possess their own individual uniqueness. That ought to tell us that our individuality is a sacred trust—and what we do with it is our gift to God. Our best contribution in life—our "utmost for his highest"—can only be made as we allow God to finish his work in progress and perfect our uniqueness. To live without discovering our uniqueness is to not really live. I think God is heartbroken when his children miss out on the potential he has placed inside of them.

Or consider what Max Lucado says about uniqueness in his book, *Cure for the Common Life*:

Da Vinci painted one *Mona Lisa*, Beethoven created one *Fifth Symphony*, and God made one version of you. You're it! You're the only you there is. And if we don't get you, we don't get you. You're the only shot we have at you. You can do something no one else can do in a fashion no one else can do it. You are more than a coincidence of chromosomes and heredity, more than just an assemblage of somebody else's lineage. You are uniquely made....

But can you be anything you want to be? If you are uniquely made—now stop and think about this—if you're uniquely made, can you really be anything you want to be? If you don't have the sense that takes care of numbers, can you be an accountant? If you don't have a love for the dirt, can you be a farmer? If you don't have an appreciation and a devotion to kids, can you really be a teacher? Well, you can be an unhappy one, an unsatisfied one. You can be one of the 87 percent of the workforce that doesn't like their work—one of the 80 percent of the people that says "I don't use my talents on a daily basis." You can be a statistic.

✳ *May*
Lucado ends his comments with these powerful words: "Can you be anything you want to be? I don't think so. But can you be everything God wants you to be? I do think so. And you do become that by discovering your uniqueness."

Friend, I hope your heart beats with anticipation and excitement knowing that God is going to start revealing your uniqueness to you as the pages ahead unfold.

Your Unique Purpose

God created you as a unique masterpiece because he has a specific purpose for your life – a specific and unique "contribution" that only you can make.

What does that mean? Your contribution is the unique service God created you to make, a ministry only you can perform. It is the specific mission God has given you to fulfill for him on earth. It is what I like to call your unique *Kingdom Purpose*.

I define Kingdom Purpose as … *your specific contribution to the body of Christ, within your generation, that causes you to totally depend on God and authentically display his love toward others – all through the expression of your unique S.H.A.P.E.* The Bible says, "Each person is given something to do that shows who God is: Everyone gets in on it, everyone benefits" (1 Corinthians 12:7, MSG).

Your Kingdom Purpose is way more than a career. It is a special commissioning from God to make a significant difference on this earth. It's the banner of your life that you carry and wave for God's glory. Now don't get me wrong, your career could provide you the platform to direct your Kingdom Purpose, but it doesn't *define* it.

I have discovered that most people, myself included, tend to define their purpose in life by one of three things … *trends*, what others *tell* them, or by *truth*. When we let trends guide our life, we simply are living to fit into the current styles of the world. When we let others tell us what we should be doing, we are living to please them and win their approval. However, when we let God's truth define our Kingdom Purpose, submitting to his authority and desiring to please only him, we are able to lead a life of lasting significance, fulfillment, and Kingdom impact.

In fact, your Kingdom Purpose is very much a reflection of your faithfulness to God. The Bible defines faith as the confident assurance that what we hope for is going to happen (see Hebrews 11:1). The more time we spend with God, the more we learn of his goodness and faithfulness – and the stronger our faith in him becomes. We learn from God's Word that it is impossible to please God without faith (see Hebrews 11:6).

That very chapter of Scripture – Hebrews 11 – lists many ordinary people who by faith accomplished extraordinary things for God, among them Noah, Abraham, Joseph, Moses, and Rahab. Over the years, I have had the privilege of personally seeing thousands of ordinary people live out their Kingdom Purpose through their confident assurance in God.

One of those people is John Baker—an ordinary man God has used in extraordinary ways. For many years, John battled an addiction to alcohol. It almost cost him his marriage, his family, and his life. Thankfully, John found God through his local church. That turning point led him to write his senior pastor a lengthy letter, outlining the vision for a ministry he believed God was nudging him to start. He also confessed his feelings of inadequacy about taking on such a task. Not long after, the pastor challenged John to go after his dream.

The next year, John launched a new ministry called Celebrate Recovery, a biblical process to help people find freedom from addictions through the love and grace of Jesus Christ. For the next ten years, God used John to deliver hundreds of people from the grip of destructive lifestyles. In 2004, President George W. Bush publicly recognized John for bringing hope to hurting people. Today, Celebrate Recovery is an international ministry helping millions of people overcome painful pasts and harmful addictions through the merciful, powerful love of Jesus.

If you were to meet John Baker, you would see an average guy who took everything God had made him to be—the positive as well as the painful—and chose to use it for God's glory. With God's help and leading, John has made and continues to make a kingdom difference by fulfilling his unique Kingdom Purpose.

God is continually looking for ordinary people such as John who are willing to let him use them to make a difference for his kingdom. From business executives to bus drivers, from teachers to techies, from stay-at-home moms to traveling musicians, from dentists to deli owners, God longs to use ordinary people in extraordinary ways. That includes *you*!

✳ Will you accept the challenge to find and carry out your Kingdom Purpose? Remember, the Bible says, "Be strong and courageous. Do not be terrified; do not be discouraged, for the LORD your God will be with you wherever you go" (Joshua 1:9).

With this encouragement, challenge yourself to invest in God's kingdom in a way that will last long after you are gone. Be a contributor, not a consumer. For some people—like John Baker—that means trading in a career for a full-time ministry. For most of us, however, finding and fulfilling our Kingdom Purpose means discovering how God wants us to minister in the paths and relationships of the daily lives he has given us. For all of us, it means determining that we will let God use us to impact eternity and leave a heavenly legacy on earth.

Your Special S.H.A.P.E.

As one of God's custom-designed creations, your potential for significance and excellence is revealed by the S.H.A.P.E. God has given you. The S.H.A.P.E. concept was developed by Rick Warren, who writes, "Whenever God gives us an assignment, he always equips us with what we need to accomplish it. This custom combination of capabilities is called your S.H.A.P.E."

The word S.H.A.P.E. points to five specific characteristics:

- **Spiritual Gifts**: A set of special abilities that God has given you to share his love and serve others.
- **Heart**: The special passions God has given you so that you can glorify him on earth.
- **Abilities**: The set of talents that God gave you when you were born, which he also wants you to use to make an impact for him.
- **Personality**: The special way God wired you to navigate life and fulfill your unique Kingdom Purpose.
- **Experiences**: Those parts of your past, both positive and painful, which God intends to use in great ways.

Rick continues:

When God created animals, he gave each of them a specific area of expertise. Some animals run, some hop, some swim, some burrow, and some fly. Each animal has a particular role to play based on the way they were shaped by God. The same is true with humans. Each of us was uniquely designed, or shaped, by God to do certain things.

Wise stewardship of your life begins by understanding your shape. You are unique, wonderfully complex, a composite of many different factors. What God made you to be determines what he intends for you to do. Your ministry is determined by your makeup.

If you don't understand your shape, you end up doing things that God never intended or designed you to do. When your gifts don't meet the role you play in life, you feel like a square peg in a round hole. This is frustrating, both to you and to others. Not only does it produce limited results, it is also an enormous waste of your talents, time, and energy.

Another assignment I remember from that college art class involved using a potter's wheel to create something from clay. I spent three weeks trying to master the use of the wheel, with little success. My pitiful excuse for a bowl resembled nothing that could be called "art." The cute girl in the class, however, *could* make beautiful pots. The clay seemed to come alive in her hands, as her skillful fingers molded it into any shape she desired. She was able to make the wheel spin at the perfect speed and apply just the right pressure to the clay.

I remember the art professor telling us that when clay is pliable it requires just a small amount of pressure to shape it. The opposite also is true—when clay is stiff and resistant, a lot more pressure is needed to mold it the way the potter desires.

That very truth is evident in a passage from the book of Jeremiah:

> The LORD gave another message to Jeremiah. He said, "Go down to the shop where clay pots and jars are made. I will speak to you while you are there." So I did as he told me and found the potter working at his wheel. But the jar he was making did not turn out as he had hoped, so the potter squashed the jar into a lump of clay and started again. Then the LORD gave me this message: "O Israel, can I not do to you as this potter has done to his clay? As the clay is in the potter's hand, so are you in my hand" (Jeremiah 18:1–6, NLT).

Here God gives us a clear, beautiful picture to explain his relationship to us. He is the master craftsman; we are like clay in his hands. His role is to carefully shape us; ours is to remain pliable, allowing him to do so. It's amazing how well the process works when we cooperate! As the prophet Isaiah emphasized: "And yet, LORD, you are our Father. We are the clay, and you are the potter. We are all formed by your hand" (Isaiah 64:8, NLT).

As we allow God's hands to lovingly mold us, we submit ourselves to his purpose in creating us. God specially designs each of us for doing his will on earth. Each one of us is intentionally shaped to fulfill the specific plan he has for each life. Understanding this amazing concept should produce in us a desire to humbly and gratefully accept the role God has created us to fill.

When we reach this position of heart—when we become pliable and welcome the loving pressure of God—we understand that his purpose is to handcraft us for a special role only we are able to fulfill.

Just Be You

If you could press a rewind button on my life, you would see that for many years I was running away from who God created me to be. I wanted to make a lot of money before making an eternal difference. I'm forever thankful to the people who helped me replace my confused and cluttered life with the clarity and confidence of God's truth. While the world shouted at me to look and live like other people, God's voice rose above all the noise with a clear message: "Erik, just be you!" Today I live with the freedom to be who God created me to be. That freedom gives me incredible focus and lasting fulfillment.

I'm not special in this regard. I believe with all my heart that God has the same message for you.

You were not created to conform. You were not created to compare. You were not created to compete. You were not created to compromise. You were created to contribute to God's kingdom and make a significant difference with your life. You were created to *just be you*!

God is saying to each of us, "Just be you. Be who I shaped you to be. I gave you new life—Christ's life—so you could make a significant difference in the world. Do what I planned for you to do. Serve beyond yourself. I'm waiting to bless your life on earth and reward your efforts in heaven." The question is, Will you receive the greatness God has for you? Will you fulfill his special assignments for your life?

As you get ready to discover and maximize your unique God-given S.H.A.P.E., I want to take you back once more to the art gallery I visited during college.

There were many famous reproductions in that studio. On one wall hung one of Henri Matisse's most important masterpieces, *The Dance*. Although Matisse had painted the theme of the dance before, only this composition reached his full passion and expressive resonance. The power of the dance is captured in a stunning frenzy of red, blue, and green – uniting man, heaven, and earth.

On another wall hung Claude Monet's masterpiece, *Water Lilies*, in which the artist experimented with the interplay of light and water. Sunlight erases the boundary between objects and their reflection. Though decorative on the surface, the *Water Lilies* series embodies a philosophy far deeper.

The last masterpiece I saw was Vincent Van Gogh's *The Starry Night*, perhaps his most loved work. The scene depicted in the painting literally jumps off the canvas – with rockets blazing yellow and planets spinning like pinwheels above hills that undulate and heave.

Now, let's imagine for a moment that a portrait of your life hangs next to these others. What does it look like? What are the unique details? What is the title? Is the canvas full of beautiful colors, or is it confused and cluttered? Would you rather see a painting of your life as it is, or would you prefer the masterpiece God wants to create?

It doesn't matter that your life doesn't look like God's masterpiece yet. Great art takes time. God's Word promises that "He who began a good work in you will perfect it until the day of Christ Jesus" (Philippians 1:6b, NASB). He promises that he will keep working on you until the artwork of your life is just as fine as that of Jesus himself! (See Ephesians 4:13.)

I hope you will launch into this discovery process with excitement and anticipation, filled with the confidence that clay or a paintbrush inspires in the hands of a master artist. Think of each of the following chapters as a specific color God will use to bring your masterpiece to life. Let him bring out the details in your life that he wants to use for his glory. As your masterpiece takes shape, see it as a gift from God – and realize that what you do with your life is your gift back to him.

Enjoy the time with your Master!

GRABBING HOLD

At the end of every chapter you will find this special section, designed to help you move from *information* (what the Bible says about you) to *application* (how you will change your life because of these truths). If you are journeying through this material with another person, this is a great place to share your learnings. And if you're going through the material with a group of people, check out Appendix 7: Grabbing Hold Together.

Furthermore, I encourage you to take advantage of the additional online S.H.A.P.E. resources available at *www.shapediscovery.com*. This interactive website is full of helpful tools, tips, and ongoing training, all dedicated to ensuring you can start finding and fulfilling your unique Kingdom Purpose.

■ ■ ■ ■ ■

Every journey has a starting point. Today is the starting point of your life-changing journey of discovery. Before you begin, take a moment to mark your starting place. Where are you today, right now, at the beginning of your adventure with God? The list below will help you mark the spot. Read each statement and indicate your current status by circling the appropriate number: 3 = yes, 2 = somewhat, 1 = no. When you have finished, add the numbers for your score.

My unique God-given purpose in life is clear.	3	2	1
My spiritual gifts are being expressed.	3	2	1
My passions are being utilized for God.	3	2	1
My natural abilities are being used to serve others.	3	2	1
My personality is helping me serve others.	3	2	1
My purpose capitalizes on many of my experiences.	3	2	1
My life is completely surrendered to God.	3	2	1
My attitude and actions reflect a servant heart.	3	2	1
My accountability to others is consistent.	3	2	1
My schedule shows how I'm investing in others.	3	2	1
My plan to fulfill my purpose from God is set.	3	2	1

Total: _____

Where Are You Today?

A Focused Kingdom Purpose (25+ points) – Based on your answers, your God-given strengths seem clear and your specific purpose from God is concise. Your life is in balance and providing lasting fulfillment. You strive to live surrendered so you can find freedom in your role as a servant. You have a solid accountability team in place that offers the encouragement and support you need to be faithful to God's design. You invest in the lives of others on a regular basis. Your master plan is on target for maximizing your God-given strengths. You feel you truly are living the life you were meant to live.

If you scored in this range, this book will help you further clarify what God has given you and give him the opportunity to affirm what you already are doing on his behalf.

A Fragmented Kingdom Purpose (15–25 points) – Based on your answers, your God-honoring purpose seems cluttered. Your strengths are somewhat confused due to the fact that you are overextended in many areas of your life – something we can all relate to. There are times when you feel you are using your gifts for God's glory, but there also are issues, emotions, and desires in your life that you still need to surrender to God in order to live the life he has in store for you. Your accountability to others may not be as consistent as God – or you – would like. You desire to invest in others, but have not committed the time. You have a few goals in place, but no master plan to ensure your purpose for God is completed. The result is intermittent fulfillment. You occasionally feel you are living the life you were created for, but you long for greater clarity.

If you find yourself here, this book will help bring greater clarity to your God-given strengths and the specific purpose for which God made you.

A Frustrated Kingdom Purpose (Less than 15 points) – Based on your answers, you are confused about your specific purpose in life for God. You lack a clear idea of who you are and you have few clues about what God made you to do. Your specific God-given strengths are unknown. Surrender and servanthood are not themes you have engaged at this stage of your journey with God. You don't feel safe making yourself accountable to others. Investing in others is not currently a priority of your life.

Overall, your life is not as balanced as you would like it to be. Fulfillment is hard for you to find. You admit you don't have a clear-cut strategy for your life. You may even feel most of the time that you are just surviving.

Many people walk through life confused. If you are here, thank God for putting a tool in your hands that will replace your confusion with his clarity and confidence.

▪ ▪ ▪ ▪ ▪

Now that you know where you are today, the next question is, Where would you like to be by the time you finish reading this book? What is the one thing you long for God to do in your life as you spend time with him?

To capture this moment, write God a note in the space below, asking him to help you see how special you are and the specific purpose he has just for you.

▪ ▪ ▪ ▪ ▪

Dear God,

_____

_____

_____

_____

_____

_____

_____

_____

(Don't forget to sign your name and date it.)

Chapter 2

SPIRITUAL GIFTS

Unwrapping Your God-Given Treasures

Now about the gifts of the Spirit, brothers and sisters,
I do not want you to be uninformed.
1 Corinthians 12:1 (TNIV)

Your spiritual gifts were not given for your own benefit
but for the benefit of others.
Rick Warren

I used to think that God's gifts were on shelves —
one above another — and the taller we grow,
the easier we can reach them.
Now I find that God's gifts are on shelves —
and the lower we stoop, the more we get.
F. B. Meyer

You have been gifted for greatness.

Is there anything more fun than watching children open Christmas presents? My wife, Stacey, and I have three children. Christmas morning in our house is wild! Our children leap out of bed at the crack of dawn and race down the stairs to see what Santa has left them under the tree. When they find presents with their names on them, bows and paper fly in every direction!

As their father, I take special pleasure in watching each one enjoy the moment. My heart is filled with love as their eyes brighten with the excitement of discovery. I am delighted when they ask me to show them how to use the gifts. ("Some assembly required. Batteries not included.") Satisfaction fills my soul as I watch them begin to actually play with these things Stacey and I picked out especially for them.

Now picture this same wonderful scene, only with spiritual gifts. When God planned the masterpiece he would make of your life, he decided to give you certain gifts that would enable you to effectively share his love and make your own unique contribution to his kingdom. He placed these spiritual abilities within you and waits eagerly for you to discover them. I'm certain it fills his heart with joy as he watches us discover and start using the spiritual gifts he has given us. We should be as excited as children on Christmas Day about unwrapping these treasures.

In his book, *19 Gifts of the Spirit*, Leslie B. Flynn writes: "You are a gifted child of God. Since you are also given an outlet for your gift, you are a minister too. For every gift he bestows, the Spirit has planned a sphere of service. Thus, no child should have an inferiority complex. Rather, awareness that he is a gifted child with an area of ministry should meet every child of God's psychological need to feel wanted and to possess a sense of worth."

Too often, I see people carrying heavy loads of frustration because they are trying to serve in areas for which they have little or no ability. On the other hand, the most fulfilled and effective people I see are functioning in areas that precisely match the gifts God has given them.

For many years, Trisha believed she was "only" a coordinator for a ministry—and she felt vaguely dissatisfied about it. Then, in her fifties, she finally understood that God had gifted her to be the team's administrator. "It seems the team functions more effectively when I use my gifts, and when others use theirs," she says. "From now on, I'm going to enjoy this wonderful opportunity to express what God has given me."

Perhaps you believe you don't have a gift at all. Brent, a lifelong member of Saddleback Church, once murmured, "I only run the computerized music program for our college ministry." But when he looked at his life through the lens of spiritual gifts, Brent realized that his gift of serving was crucial to the success of the college ministry.

Or maybe you are like Jeff and Joy, who said to me, "We are just parents. We don't have a lot of time to make a contribution with our lives right now." When they learned God had given them gifts of encouragement, leadership, administration, and mercy, they were thrilled to realize God had shaped them to help their four children become everything God planned for them to be.

Understanding Spiritual Gifts

At first, this whole issue of spiritual gifts may seem mysterious, complicated, and difficult—but in fact the opposite is true. God has given us wonderful gifts, and he doesn't make it difficult to discover and use them.

In 1 Corinthians 12:1, Paul says, "Now about spiritual gifts, brothers, I do not want you to be ignorant." The word *ignorant* here does not mean "unintelligent" or "naive." Rather, Paul is telling us that if we are uninformed, we will miss out on the wonderful gifts God has given us. Your heavenly Father wants his children to be fully informed so they can unwrap every single gift they have received. Your gifts are the key to fulfilling the Kingdom Purpose he has set aside just for you. When that truth finally sank in for me, it was sobering. Suddenly I felt a deep desire to understand the entire subject of spiritual gifts.

As a pastor, I hear several questions about spiritual gifts that come up over and over. As we examine what the Bible says, we discover God's answers to those questions.

What Are Spiritual Gifts?

Let's start by clarifying what they are not. First, your spiritual gifts are not the same as your personality traits. A personality test is not an adequate indicator of what spiritual gifts you possess. Your personality traits, however, do provide natural vehicles for expressing your gifts. For example, if God wired you to be outgoing, then your gifts will work best as you actively engage other people. If you are more reserved by nature, your personality will complement your giftedness.

Second, spiritual gifts are not the same as natural talents. You can be a very talented architect, salesperson, or manager, but those are not spiritual gifts. Leslie B. Flynn explains, "Talents have to do with techniques and methods; gifts have to do with spiritual abilities. Talents depend on natural power, gifts on spiritual endowment."

Third, spiritual gifts are not the same as the fruit of the Spirit described in Galatians 5:22–23: love, joy, peace, patience, kindness, goodness, faithfulness, gentleness, and self-control. The fruit of the Spirit reveal Christ's contribution to our character, while our spiritual gifts reveal the contribution we make to God's kingdom.

So what *are* spiritual gifts? For this study, let's define a spiritual gift as *a God-given special ability, given to every believer at conversion by the Holy Spirit, to share his love and strengthen the body of Christ.* The Bible tells us in 1 Peter 4:10 that God is the gift giver: "God has given gifts to each of you from his great variety of spiritual gifts. Manage them well so that God's generosity can flow through you" (NLT).

I love how Os Guinness, in his book *The Call*, talks about the role of giftedness. Os says, "The purpose of giftedness is stewardship and service, not selfishness."

God gives us these special abilities for specific reasons. Spiritual gifts only work in spiritual ways. Designed to bring great color and clarity to your life, they can only be used to their full potential when empowered by the Holy Spirit, who dwells in the life of every believer. Only those who have entered into a personal relationship with Christ have these gifts.

Why Does God Give Spiritual Gifts?

In 1 Corinthians 12:7, Paul says, "A spiritual gift is given to each of us as a means of helping the entire church" (NLT). The spiritual gifts God gives you are neither *for you* nor *about you*. They weren't given to boost your self-image or to serve as some kind of special reward from God. They were not given to raise you up to some level of worldly greatness or success. They are yours for the express purpose of blessing the body of Christ—the church. That is why you need to be part of a church family. Discovering your spiritual gifts is not the ultimate goal—using them to bless others is.

Does Everyone Get a Gift?

The Bible assures us that every believer receives gifts from God: "Each of you has your own gift from God; one has this gift, another has that" (1 Corinthians 7:7b, TNIV). You may not feel tremendously gifted, but God says that you are. Every Christian has at least one spiritual gift.

In my role as pastor of ministry and S.H.A.P.E. discovery at Saddleback, I have seen that people discover their gifts as they minister to others. The more you serve God in ministry, the more clearly you will see your gifts.

God gives gifts to everyone, not just "special" people. There are no special qualifications needed, no special level of maturity required, not even a particular time span needed in your journey with Jesus. *If you are a believer, then you have the Spirit living in you. If you have the Spirit living in you, then you have spiritual gifts to use for God's glory and the benefit of others.*

(If you are reading this and aren't sure you have a personal relationship with God, please turn to Appendix 3: The Best Gift Ever, so you can be certain that you do.)

You may not have discovered the gifts you have or begun to use them yet, but you definitely have them. You have God's word on it. He is the one who decided which gifts to give you. *How many* gifts you have is not nearly as important as discovering and developing the gifts you do have.

When we use what God has graced us with, people are helped, he is honored, and we are fulfilled. As mentioned before, the best place to explore your giftedness is at your church—the body of Christ in which God has placed you. If you aren't involved with a local church, I strongly suggest you find one so you can experience the many blessings that come from being part of a church family.

Unwrapping Spiritual Gifts

Perhaps you now understand for the very first time the great importance of spiritual gifts. But understanding without experiencing is like seeing presents under the Christmas tree but never opening them. Actually unwrapping your spiritual gifts will help you see the masterpiece God has created you to be and discover the wonderful ways he has made it possible for you to live a meaningful life of service to others.

The key to discovering your gifts is twofold: (1) examining what gifts you think you may have, and then (2) serving in various roles to see which ones bring the greatest fulfillment for you and the greatest results for God. Taking tests designed to identify your gifts and abilities cannot take the place of actually experimenting with different types of service. Rick Warren says, "Many books get the discovery process backwards. They say, 'Discover your spiritual gift and then you'll know what ministry you're supposed to have.' It actually works the exact opposite way. Just start serving, experimenting with different ministries, and then you'll discover your gifts. Until you're actually involved in serving, you're not going to know what you're good at."

So let's begin by recognizing what God identifies as spiritual gifts. To do so, we need to look at five passages of Scripture:

> We have different gifts, according to the grace given us. If a man's gift is prophesying, let him use it in proportion to his faith. If it is serving, let him serve; if it is teaching, let him teach; if it is encouraging, let him encourage; if it is contributing to the needs of others, let him give generously; if it is leadership, let him govern diligently; if it is showing mercy, let him do it cheerfully (Romans 12:6–8).

> To one there is given through the Spirit the message of wisdom, to another the message of knowledge by means of the same Spirit, to another faith by the same Spirit, to another gifts of healing by that one Spirit, to another miraculous powers, to another prophecy, to another distinguishing between spirits, to another speaking in different kinds of tongues, and to still another the interpretation of tongues (1 Corinthians 12:8–10).

> And in the church God has appointed first of all apostles, second prophets, third teachers, then workers of miracles, also those having

gifts of healing, those able to help others, those with gifts of administration, and those speaking in different kinds of tongues (1 Corinthians 12:28).

It was he who gave some to be apostles, some to be prophets, some to be evangelists, and some to be pastors and teachers (Ephesians 4:11).

Offer hospitality to one another without grumbling. Each one should use whatever gift he has received to serve others, faithfully administering God's grace in its various forms (1 Peter 4:9–10).

From these passages, we can pull together a list of twenty spiritual gifts:

Administration	Interpretation
Apostleship	Knowledge
Discernment	Leadership
Encouragement	Mercy
Evangelism	Miracles
Faith	Pastoring
Giving	Prophecy
Healing	Teaching
Helping	Tongues
Hospitality	Wisdom

As you reach out to take hold of your gifts, allow Scripture to guide you to those that are uniquely yours. Ask God to reveal how he wants you to use your gifts to accomplish his work in the world. As you do this, you may discover that what you thought was a self-guided desire is in fact a reflection of the spiritual gifts God has given you.

Perhaps you are like Becky, who didn't see that she had gifts that served a legitimate purpose. Once the S.H.A.P.E. lens brought into focus her spiritual gifts of mercy, encouragement, and shepherding, she discovered a significant and fulfilling ministry in counseling others.

Then there is Seth, who realized that his long-buried dream of serving in full-time ministry was in fact a reflection of the spiritual gifts of teaching, leadership, and pastoring. Or perhaps you will identify with Debbie, who took on the role as the director of women's ministries at her church when she learned how valuable her gifts of leadership, pastoring, and encouragement were to others.

Unwrapping *Your* Spiritual Gifts

To help you get started in discovering your own spiritual gifts, review the following explanations for each of the twenty gifts listed on page 37.

As you read each definition, think back on your own experience in serving Christ. Then indicate "yes" if you feel you have this gift, "maybe" if you might have this gift, or "no" if you don't think you have this gift. When your findings are complete, transfer them to your S.H.A.P.E. *for* Life Profile in Appendix 1 on pages 221–223.

Administration: The God-given special ability to serve and strengthen the body of Christ by effectively organizing resources and people in order to efficiently reach ministry goals. Individuals with this gift …

- Are effective organizers of people and projects toward reaching ministry goals.
- Are known for having specific plans to achieve clearly defined goals.
- Naturally delegate tasks, making it possible to accomplish more for God's kingdom.
- Seek decision-making opportunities.
- Understand what needs to be done for dreams to become a reality.

□ Yes   □ Maybe   □ No

Apostleship: The God-given special ability to serve and strengthen the body of Christ by launching and leading new ministry ventures that advance God's purposes and expand his kingdom. The original Greek meaning of the word is "sent one" (literally, one sent with authority, or as an ambassador). People with this gift …

- Are driven to start new endeavors for God, most often churches.
- Often welcome risky new challenges.
- Enjoy making a difference in the lives of believers and unbelievers alike.

- Are eager to be known as ambassadors for Christ in the world.
- Willingly work hard to see churches reach their full potential for God.

☐ Yes   ☐ Maybe   ☐ No

Discernment: The God-given special ability to serve and strengthen the body of Christ by recognizing truth or error within a message, person, or event. People with this gift ...

- Find it easy to "read" others, and are most often right.
- Recognize the spiritual source of a message—whether it is from God, Satan, or man.
- Recognize inconsistencies in others.
- Easily identify people's true motives and agendas.
- Perceive when the truth is twisted or communicated with error.

☐ Yes   ☐ Maybe   ☐ No

Encouragement: The God-given special ability to serve and strengthen the body of Christ by helping others live God-centered lives through inspiration, encouragement, counseling, and empowerment. People with this gift ...

- Are driven to inspire others and impact their lives positively for Christ.
- Rejoice with those whose reliance on Christ has helped them overcome difficult life situations.
- Seek out opportunities to help others reach their full potential in Christ.
- Are natural encouragers, whether in words or through actions.
- Rejoice at others' success.

☐ Yes   ☐ Maybe   ☐ No

Evangelism: The God-given special ability to serve and strengthen the body of Christ by sharing the love of Christ with others in a way that draws them to respond by accepting God's free gift of eternal life. People with this gift ...

- Look for ways to build relational bridges with nonbelievers.
- Sense when a person is open to Christ's message.
- Have likely seen many people come to faith in Jesus.
- Win others to Christ through the use of love over logic.
- Are deeply burdened for those who don't know Jesus.

☐ Yes ☐ Maybe ☐ No

Faith: The God-given special ability to serve and strengthen the body of Christ by stepping out in faith in order to see God's purposes accomplished, trusting him to handle any and all obstacles along the way. People with this gift ...

- Welcome risk for God.
- Are energized by variables.
- Are challenged by ideas most see as impossible.
- Are often characterized by a passionate prayer life.
- Have great God-confidence in their ventures.

☐ Yes ☐ Maybe ☐ No

Giving: The God-given special ability to serve and strengthen the body of Christ by joyfully supporting and funding various kingdom initiatives through material contributions beyond the tithe. People with this gift ...

- Plan and purposely give over and above the 10 percent tithe, in order to see God's kingdom advanced.
- Generally prefer that their donations remain anonymous or low-profile.
- Strategically seek out ways to increase their resources, in order to contribute more for God's use.
- See their resources as tools for God's use.
- Recognize God's ultimate ownership of everything.

☐ Yes ☐ Maybe ☐ No

Healing: The God-given special ability to serve and strengthen the body of Christ by healing and restoring to health, beyond traditional and natural means, those who are sick, hurting, and suffering. People with this gift ...

- Believe firmly that people can be supernaturally healed.
- Pray specifically to be used by God to heal others.
- Fully realize that healing occurs only by God's divine permission.
- View medicine as a means God may choose for healing.
- Embrace their gift as from the hand of God, and as a specific way to bring him glory.

☐ Yes   ☐ Maybe   ☐ No

Helping: The God-given special ability to serve and strengthen the body of Christ by offering others assistance in reaching goals that glorify God and strengthen the body of Christ. This aptitude is sometimes referred to as the gift of "helps" or "service." People with this gift ...

- Enjoy and seek out ways to serve behind the scenes.
- Rejoice in the success of others.
- Are often detail-oriented.
- Look for ways to be of assistance to others.
- Do not seek recognition for their efforts.

☐ Yes   ☐ Maybe   ☐ No

Hospitality: The God-given special ability to serve and strengthen the body of Christ by providing others with a warm and welcoming environment for fellowship. People with this gift ...

- Are known for making those around them feel valued and cared for.
- Look for those individuals who may go unnoticed in a crowd.
- Desire that people feel loved and welcomed.
- See their home as God's property, given to them expressly to make others feel welcome.
- Promote fellowship among others wherever they are.

☐ Yes   ☐ Maybe   ☐ No

Interpretation: The God-given special ability to serve and strengthen the body of Christ by understanding, at a specific time, God's message when spoken by another using a special language unknown to the others in attendance. People with this gift tend to ...

- Have a clear idea of what God is saying, even though the language used by the speaker is unknown to them at the specific time.
- Be able to translate words and messages of God in a way that edifies, comforts, and exhorts believers.
- Convey the meaning of sounds, words, and utterances that glorify God, made by others.

☐ Yes ☐ Maybe ☐ No

Knowledge: The God-given special ability to serve and strengthen the body of Christ by communicating God's truth to others in a way that promotes justice, honesty, and understanding. People with this gift ...

- Devote much of their time to reading Scripture.
- Love to share biblical insight.
- Enjoy helping others increase their understanding of God's Word.
- Benefit from time spent in studying and researching Scripture.
- Take delight in answering difficult questions about God's Word.

☐ Yes ☐ Maybe ☐ No

Leadership: The God-given special ability to serve and strengthen the body of Christ by casting vision, stimulating spiritual growth, applying strategies, and achieving success where God's purposes are concerned. People with this gift ...

- Exhibit a tendency toward huge visions for God and the ability to inspire others to work toward accomplishing those visions for his glory, and to bless others.
- Are naturally drawn into leadership roles.
- Find it easy to motivate people — both individually and in teams — to work together in achieving goals for God's kingdom.
- Naturally grasp the "big picture."

- Are able to let go of responsibility and delegate it to others who are qualified.

  ☐ Yes   ☐ Maybe   ☐ No

Mercy: The God-given special ability to serve and strengthen the body of Christ by ministering to those who suffer physically, emotionally, spiritually, or relationally. Their actions are characterized by love, care, compassion, and kindness toward others. People with this gift ...

- Are drawn toward opportunities to practically meet the needs of others.
- Devote significant time in prayer for the needs of others.
- Tend to place the needs of others ahead of their own.
- Grieve with those who grieve.
- Are most fulfilled when visiting people in need – in hospitals, nursing homes, prisons, orphanages, villages, or wherever God directs them.

  ☐ Yes   ☐ Maybe   ☐ No

Miracles: The God-given special ability to serve and strengthen the body of Christ through supernatural acts that bring validity to God and his power. People with this gift ...

- Recognize prayer as a supernatural vehicle through which God acts in the lives of people on earth.
- Render credit and thanks to God alone for supernatural works.
- Fully grasp the fact that miracles only occur when God wills them to happen.
- See themselves as instruments for God's use.
- Pray and look to supernatural results whenever they encounter impossible life situations.

  ☐ Yes   ☐ Maybe   ☐ No

Pastoring: The God-given special ability to serve and strengthen the body of Christ by taking spiritual responsibility for a group of believers and equipping them to live Christ-centered lives. Shepherding is another word used for this particular gift. You could have this gift if you ...

- Are driven to help others reach their full potential in Christ.
- Enjoy serving others and look for opportunities to do this.
- Are good at developing personal, trust-based relationships with a small number of people.
- Have a propensity toward meeting the needs of others, willingly giving your time to help them with spiritual issues.
- Believe that people take precedence over projects.

☐ Yes   ☐ Maybe   ☐ No

Prophecy: The God-given special ability to serve and strengthen the body of Christ by offering messages from God that comfort, encourage, guide, warn, or reveal sin in a way that leads to repentance and spiritual growth. The original Greek meaning of this word is "to speak forth the truth." The gift of prophecy includes both "forth telling" (preaching), and "foretelling" (revelation). You may have this gift if you ...

- Are known for publicly communicating God's Word, using a variety of means.
- Love to share your strong biblical convictions with others.
- View yourself as God's tool, ready to be used by the Holy Spirit in changing lives.
- Find it easy to confront others' motives when they are not up to God's standards.
- Frequently receive and share messages directly from God for comforting, challenging, and confronting his people.

☐ Yes   ☐ Maybe   ☐ No

Teaching: The God-given special ability to serve and strengthen the body of Christ by teaching sound doctrine in relevant ways, empowering people to gain a sound and mature spiritual education. Individuals who have this gift ...

- Are given to hours in the study of Scripture in order to best apply its principles and truth.
- Enjoy making the Bible clear and understandable to others.
- Seek out opportunities to speak biblical insight into daily situations.

- Are good at helping others learn to study the Bible.
- Recognize a variety of ways to effectively communicate the Word of God, including speaking.

  ☐ Yes   ☐ Maybe   ☐ No

Tongues: The God-given special ability to serve and strengthen the body of Christ by communicating God's message in a special language unknown to the speaker. People with this gift tend to ...

- Believe God is prompting them to communicate his message, often through prayer, in a specific language unknown to them.
- Intercede for others in prayer using unknown words, sounds, and utterances.
- Desire opportunities to pray, using these unknown languages for God's glory.
- Share with others words and/or messages of God given to them using unknown languages.
- Comfort or exhort others using unknown languages inspired by God.

  ☐ Yes   ☐ Maybe   ☐ No

Wisdom: The God-given special ability to serve and strengthen the body of Christ by making wise decisions and counseling others with sound advice, all in accordance with God's will. You may possess this gift if you ...

- Enjoy speaking biblical insights into life situations.
- Are sought after by others for advice/wisdom.
- Take pleasure in counseling others.
- Are known for making correct decisions and judgments.
- Recognize God as the primary source of wisdom and direction.

  ☐ Yes   ☐ Maybe   ☐ No

Now list the gifts you feel you may have (the "yes" and "maybe" ones) in your S.H.A.P.E. *for* Life Profile in Appendix 1 on pages 221–223.

Sharing Your Spiritual Gifts

Now that you have identified some possible spiritual gifts God has given you, start to express them by serving others around you. When we serve in areas that best match our giftedness, we experience great(er) fulfillment and see great(er) fruitfulness for God. On the other hand, when we serve outside our giftedness, we usually end up frustrated and fatigued. Serving others is the best way to clarify your giftedness because it allows you the opportunity to try out your gifts.

That is why we should aspire to serve in whatever way God has designed us to serve, rather than being driven by ambition to achieve what we think are great goals. Helen Keller once said, "I long to accomplish a great and noble task, but it is my chief duty to accomplish humble tasks as though they were great and noble. The world is moved along, not only by the mighty shoves of its heroes, but also by the aggregate of the tiny pushes of each honest worker."

The apostle Paul says giftedness should be expressed in love. Whenever he talks about spiritual gifts, he follows with a message about love. For example, 1 Corinthians 12 and 14 talk about spiritual gifts, but right smack-dab between these two chapters, Paul wrote what has become regarded as the definitive message regarding love:

> If I speak in the tongues of men and of angels, but have not love, I am only a resounding gong or a clanging cymbal. If I have the gift of prophecy and can fathom all mysteries and all knowledge, and if I have a faith that can move mountains, but have not love, I am nothing. If I give all I possess to the poor and surrender my body to the flames, but have not love, I gain nothing (1 Corinthians 13:1–3).

Do you see the importance of love when it comes to using our gifts for God? Paul tells us we may have wonderful and valuable spiritual gifts, but without love we are unusable. To determine what is truly propelling your spiritual gifts, ask yourself, "Who is the primary beneficiary of my actions?" If your actions benefit others, you are serving with love. If you realize *you* are the prime beneficiary of your actions, you need to immediately realign yourself with God. A love-driven life is the life God uses.

In his book, *Why You Can't Be Anything You Want to Be*, Arthur F. Miller Jr. talks about the danger of misusing what God has given us. "The dark side of giftedness means inflating its payoff beyond its intention until it has assumed the place of God."

Miller goes on to say, "Unchecked, giftedness is powerful enough to subvert entire systems to the darker purposes of the human heart. This is the real source of systemic evil." Don't fall into this trap. Rather, let love empower your gifts for the blessing of others and building up of the body of Christ.

Indeed, as you start to bless others through your spiritual gifts, you need to be aware of four common traps Satan often uses to trip up believers and make them ineffective.

Trap #1: Comparison

The first pitfall is *comparison*. This happens when we place greater value on the more visible gifts – those more likely to shine in the spotlight, such as leadership or teaching. If we have those gifts and compare ourselves with others, the result can be a prideful spirit. If we compare ourselves to others who have more visible gifts, we may feel we lack significance. Both are signs that our hearts need a serious love tune-up. Just because a gift is more visible does not guarantee it's more valuable.

Evangelism is an area of giftedness that often invites comparison. People with this gift have the ability to bring many people to faith in Christ. Believers who do not have this gift may feel inadequate by comparison. I am a case in point. My best friend clearly has the gift of evangelism and regularly shares stories of how he is using it to bring others into the family of God. Because my "numbers" weren't as high as my friend's, I believed I was letting God down.

Eventually, I realized I didn't have the specific gift of evangelism. I learned I needed to continue using my gift of *encouragement* as a way to reach out and help people find God. If I had ignored my own spiritual gift because I saw it as unimportant compared to my friend's gift, I would have made myself unavailable to God – and missed out on opportunities to be used by him.

There are no second-rate masterpieces hanging in God's art gallery. Some roles may be less glamorous than others, and self-glorifying people may sniff in disdain at certain kinds of service, but God's Word says *all* the parts of the body of Christ depend on each other: "The eye can never say to the hand, 'I don't need you.' The head can't say to the feet, 'I don't need you.' In fact, some of the parts that seem weakest and least important are really the most necessary" (1 Corinthians 12:21–22, NLT). None of us should delude ourselves into thinking that the other members of the body of Christ exist to serve us, or that others are important and we are not.

Trap #2: Projection

The second trap is *projection*. When we expect others to be good at the same things we excel at, we're "projecting" our gifts onto them. Projection is especially common in relationships at work, or even at home. For example, I have the gift of administration. If I project that gift onto others and automatically expect them to be organized and punctual at all times, feelings of frustration and resentment can set in and cause the relationship to become strained.

That is exactly what Satan wants. On the other hand, I can choose to celebrate the unique gifts God gives to others and encourage each person to be who God created them to be—which is exactly what God wants.

Trap #3: Rejection

Another common pitfall we encounter is refusing to accept the gifts God has given us. This is the trap of *rejection*. I see this more often when working with people who clearly have the gift of pastoring or shepherding, but won't acknowledge it, often because they don't have the "right" title or official position.

My chiropractor Jeff once said to me, "I'm not a pastor like you, so I can't have the gift of pastoring." Because he felt inadequate, he accepted his lack of position as evidence of a fact—but that "fact" was, in fact, *not* a fact at all. Rejection is one of Satan's favorite mind games, because it keeps us from becoming all God has planned for us. Jeff needed to embrace the *truth* of his giftedness given by God. A few months after our conversation, I saw Jeff after a weekend service and his face glowed with joy. He had taken a step of faith and, with his wife, began leading a small group at his home. He loved the opportunity to encourage, counsel, help, and pray with the ten people in his group. He had finally accepted the fact that he had the gift of pastoring and didn't need the *title* of pastor to express it.

Allowing someone else's opinion to stop you from seizing and sharing your gifts will create nothing but disappointment and sorrow in your heart. Give yourself permission to be who God gifted you to be, regardless of what others have said.

Trap #4: Deception

The final trap Satan uses is *deception*. He manipulates you into believing you have certain gifts that God in fact has not given you—distracting you from putting your true gifts into effect and preventing you from accomplishing what God intended for your life. This deception especially plays itself out when it comes to leadership. John Maxwell has said, "If you think you are a leader, but no one is following you—you are just taking a walk." People like that often expect results that will be blessed by God, yet God never meant for them to be a leader—at least not in the way they imagine.

Be wary of Satan's deception as you begin to share the gifts God has given you. Focus on God so he can reveal the spiritual gifts he has for you and show you how he wants you to use them for his glory. An excellent way to ensure that you don't fall prey to one of these traps is to ask trustworthy people in your life for help and accountability.

Strengthening Your Spiritual Gifts

In *The Purpose Driven® Life*, Rick Warren talks about the importance of developing the gifts God has given us: "Whatever gifts you have been given can be enlarged and developed through practice. For instance, no one gets the gift of teaching fully developed. But with study, feedback, and practice, a 'good' teacher can become a *better* teacher, and with time, grow to be a *master* teacher. Don't settle for a half-developed gift. Stretch yourself and learn all you can."

All of us can practice and improve our ability to use our gifts. If you have the gift of teaching, make a point of learning new teaching techniques. If leadership is part of your unique gift mix, learn how to be the best servant-leader around. If you are strong on hospitality or mercy or pastoral counsel, seek new ways to include, care for, and help others. If your life is pointing toward administration, sharpen that gift through additional training.

Don't wait to begin using your spiritual gifts until you understand all the details about how they will be expressed in your life. In *Seizing Your Divine Moment*, Erwin McManus says: "Don't look for God to fill in all the blanks. Don't wait for Him to remove all the uncertainty. Realize He may actually increase the uncertainty and leverage all the odds against you, just so you will know in the end that it wasn't your gifts but His power through your gifts that fulfilled His purpose in your life."

The apostle Paul uses a great word picture to show the importance of strengthening what God has given us when he tells young Timothy to "fan into flame" his gift (2 Timothy 1:6). Imagine smoldering embers that burst into flame as you fan them. This is exactly what happens when you develop the gifts God has given you—they become more powerful and purposeful for God and eventually boost your Kingdom Purpose like nothing else.

You have been gifted for greatness—in service, not status. Identifying your spiritual gifts is the crucial first step to finding the unique role God intends for you to fulfill. Now that you have begun to recognize your unique gifts, you need to hear from God about how he wants you to put them to work. In the next chapter, we'll take a closer look at hearing God's voice—by listening with your heart.

GRABBING · HOLD

Reflect on what you have learned. What did this chapter show you about spiritual gifts?

Realize what you have been given. What spiritual gifts do you believe God has given you?

Request help from others. What two sources of wisdom can you seek help from to discover your spiritual gifts?

Respond in faith. Identify two action steps you can take in the next month to unwrap your gifts and start using them with others. (Hint: Start by serving those closest to you!)

1. _____

   _____

2. _____

   _____

Chapter 3

HEART

Discovering Your True Passion

The core problem is not that we are too passionate about bad things,
but that we are not passionate enough about good things.
Larry Crabb, *Finding God*

Passion is the fuel of life. It is the great source of energy and drive.
It's what makes us explore new vistas, develop new relationships,
and seek solutions to perplexing problems.
Bob Buford, *Halftime*

Let your heart beat for God!

Kay Warren was living the dream. She had three great kids, two wonderful grandkids, and a comfortable home in Southern California's upscale Orange County. The daughter of a pastor, she and her husband, Rick, had cofounded one of the largest congregations in the United States. He had written a million-copy bestselling book. She was a Bible teacher, a popular speaker, and coauthor of a curriculum that teaches the essential truths of the Christian faith. She was, in her own words, the stereotypical "white, suburban soccer mom."

That all came crashing down in 2002.

Thumbing through a magazine at home, she turned a page and froze in horror at photos of African people ravaged by AIDS—children and adults with skeletal bodies whose eyes were covered in flies because they were too weak to brush them away. A box on the page said: "12 million children orphaned in Africa due to AIDS." "That was a shocking statistic to me because I didn't know a single orphan, and I couldn't believe there were twelve million orphans anywhere due to anything," Kay said.

When a month had passed and the images still haunted her, Kay realized she had come to a crossroads. She could either return to her comfortable life or hear the cries of the suffering and let her heart be engaged.

"I made a conscious decision to open my heart to the pain," she said. "When I did, God broke my heart. He shattered it in a million pieces, and I cried for days."

She cried in shame because the AIDS pandemic had been building for two decades and she'd done nothing. She also cried because God allowed her to feel the suffering those with AIDS felt. "I had no agenda. I wasn't thinking about anyone else's response but my own," she says. "I knew I couldn't stand before God when he called me home and look him in the face and tell him, 'Yes, I knew about the suffering of millions of people, but I did nothing about it.'"

She knew that obeying God would be hard. Other people—out of ignorance and fear—would reject her passion. She was afraid of contracting the disease or being seen as weak on moral issues. But she told her Lord: "If you ask my life, if that is what you ask to bring awareness, then I'll give it. That is what it will require … a willingness to give at any cost."

Kay began reading about AIDS and talking with experts. She attended conferences on HIV and AIDS. She was mesmerized by the testimony of Bruce and Darlene Marie Wilkinson, who had moved to South Africa to serve the poor. She traveled to Africa to witness the devastation first-hand. She met Flora, a woman who was dying in the same home that her unfaithful husband, his mistress, and the mistress's baby also were dying—all of AIDS. She held Flora's three-year-old daughter. "God, where is the mommy who gets to sing to her at night?" she cried. "Where is the daddy who gets to throw her into the air?"

God broke Kay's heart, and now it throbs with passion for forty million people around the world who are afflicted with HIV/AIDS. She and Rick created Acts of Mercy, a foundation that "cares for hurting people the way Jesus did." She travels the world, taking advantage of every opportunity, challenging Christians to bring relief in Jesus' name to those in pain, sorrow, poverty, and illness.

"Today, I'm a woman seriously disturbed about the HIV/AIDS pandemic sweeping our world," she say. "God has changed my heart and revolutionized my dreams."

The Bible says, "Whatever you do, work at it with all your heart, as working for the Lord, not for men, since you know that you will receive an inheritance from the Lord as a reward. It is the Lord Christ you are serving" (Colossians 3:23–24). God wants your heart to beat only for him. The ultimate contribution God has for you to make aligns with the passions he has given you for his kingdom. Identifying your passions reveals another aspect of the masterpiece God is creating in your life.

My friend Tom Paterson writes in his book, *Living the Life You Were Meant to Live*:

> Heart is where you are centered, where you desire to serve, the altar upon which you wish to place your talents. Giftedness is what you are. Heart is where you will most likely apply what you are. Heart refers to empathy, attraction, or "draw" towards a group of people, a field of expertise, or a particular type of service. Evaluating your heart

helps you determine where you might best use gifts, where you wish to serve, and whom you wish to serve.

Our hearts reflect our dreams and desires. The key is to learn how to unlock the potential within our hearts so that they can beat fully for God.

Letting Your Heart Beat for God

Rick Warren puts it well in *The Purpose Driven® Life*:

> Physically, each of us has a unique heartbeat, just as we each have unique thumbprints, eye prints, and voice prints.... It's amazing that, out of all the billions of people who have ever lived, no one has had a heartbeat exactly like yours.
>
> In the same way, God has given each of us a unique *emotional* "heartbeat" that races when we think about the subjects, activities, or circumstances that interest us. We instinctively care about some things and not about others. These reveal the nature of your heart ... [and] are clues to where you should be serving.

Kay Warren could be the prototype for anyone who wants to learn about hearts that beat for God. In her story I see five passion principles that can inspire us to dream big and think beyond our fears, in the process discovering our own unique, emotional heartbeats for God. They are:

1. Know what drives you.

   For Kay Warren, that is God and her desire to use everything he has given her to bring glory to his name every day of her life.

2. Know who you care about.

   For Warren, it clearly includes those impacted by HIV/AIDS.

3. Know the needs you will meet.

   For Warren, it includes spiritual, emotional, and physical needs.

4. Know the cause you will help conquer.

   For Warren, it is the desire to dramatically decrease the spread of HIV/AIDS in the world through care, education, and medicine.

5. Know your ultimate dream for God's kingdom.
   For Warren, her dream is to help eradicate HIV/AIDS it in her lifetime.

Now let's explore each of those principles in more detail.

What Drives You?

Because God is driving her life, Kay Warren is hoping to slow the pandemic of HIV/AIDS in the world. God is the ultimate driver of your life too—and you can experience the thrill of seeing him accomplish his best through you!

The key is to discover the cravings the Creator has put in you; often they lie deep within your spirit and you've never before taken the time or effort to identify them. Listen for the whispers of secret prayers and desires, the deep yearnings in your life. Sadly, for many people, those passions go unexpressed, at least in terms of serving in the unique role God has for them.

Ask yourself:

- What do my dreams and desires drift toward?
- What do I really want to do for God?
- What motivates me to take action?
- What do I crave?

One passion that drives my life is helping people discover who God has created them to be. I live for that. This drive keeps me focused on fulfilling my specific Kingdom Purpose for God.

Or consider Kimberly. Because she had always been a good listener, friends and family often remarked that she'd make a great counselor, and so she had seriously considered becoming a therapist. But after she became a Christian, she wondered what God wanted her to do. That's when a woman at her church encouraged her to consider serving God through counseling. Kimberly now uses her passion to reach out to—and care for—the people God brings into her path. Her ability to connect with college-aged adults makes her a natural in ministering to them.

Prior to discovering her area of service for God, Kimberly admits she was wrapped up in herself and the details of her own life—like most of us are. It's natural for us to initially ask, "How does this purpose benefit me?" with little or no regard for how it relates to others. Kimberly sees things differently now, thanks to her willingness to view life through the eyes of Christ. Today, she is likely to evaluate situations not by asking "How will this help *me*?" but by asking "What can I do to help *you* more?"

God's purposes in our lives unfold as we open ourselves to his possibilities. We begin to see the shape of his masterpiece in our lives when we identify and focus on the passions he has placed in our hearts. Of course, because we don't yet see the whole picture, we need to use what God already has revealed. As a mentor for young adult women, Kimberly has ample opportunity to use her S.H.A.P.E. – and specifically her heart – as she strives to clarify her ultimate Kingdom Purpose.

Who Do You Care About?

When the great nineteenth-century preacher Dwight L. Moody was in London during one of his famous evangelistic tours, several British clergymen visited him wanting to know his secret. How – and more specifically, *why* – was this poorly educated American so effective in winning throngs of people to Christ?

Moody took the men to the window of his hotel room and asked each in turn to tell him what they saw. One by one, the men described the people in the park below. Then Moody looked out the window, and tears began coursing down his cheeks. "What do you see, Mr. Moody?" one of the men asked.

Moody replied: "I see countless thousands of souls that will one day spend eternity in hell if they do not find the Savior."

Because he saw eternal souls where others saw only people strolling in a park, Moody approached life with a different agenda. Clearly, Moody's target audience was the lost.

God has placed people in your life who he wants you to help him reach. So the question facing you becomes, "Who is God nudging me to help, and how could he use my particular gifts to reach them?" You may feel drawn to people who are spiritually apathetic, those facing marital conflict, or those who simply need Jesus in their lives. You may be called to help teenagers make sound choices for their lives. Perhaps you are driven to make an impact on a specific demographic or age group, such as those in the business world, married couples, young children, or the elderly.

Ask yourself:

- Who do I feel I can most profoundly influence for God?
- What age range do I feel led to minister to?
- What affinity group do I feel led to serve?
- How could I impact them in a way that maximizes my gifts?

What Needs Will You Meet?

Once you define your target audience, you need to determine which needs you intend to meet in the lives of those individuals. No matter how gifted or driven you are, you can't meet every need within your target group. I would encourage you to start by focusing on the needs that God and others have met in your own life.

The Bible says, "He comforts us in all our troubles so that we can comfort others. When others are troubled, we will be able to give them the same comfort God has given us" (2 Corinthians 1:4, NLT).

Maybe there's a painful experience in your past, something God has helped you overcome. He can use our suffering, weaknesses, and failures —as well as our strengths and passions—as part of the masterpiece he is creating. Your suffering could drive you to connect with others who are suffering from similar experiences. For example, because others helped me discover my own worth and potential in Christ, I now love to help others realize their potential. That excitement about my own discovery makes me want to see others experience the same transformation.

I also love to encourage and help people who were either physically or emotionally abused as a child, because I grew up facing similar abuse. Who better to help people overcome difficulties and grow with Christ than someone who has been through the same trouble, yet has bravely moved past it? We will talk about this in much greater detail in chapter 6.

Because there are so many different kinds of needs to be met, you need to narrow your focus. Consider several primary categories:

Spiritual Needs —These typically focus on the spiritual condition of a person's life. Those who feel led to meet these types of needs long to help people discover Christ and reach their full potential in him. People who lean toward meeting these types of needs tend to use the gifts of teaching, wisdom, evangelism, knowledge, and prophecy.

Physical Needs—People with physical needs appreciate practical expressions of love. Those who focus on meeting physical needs use their resources to make sure people in need have food, clothing, shelter, and other simple necessities. The spiritual gifts of giving, helps, healing, administration, hospitality, pastoring, and mercy are most often used to meet physical needs.

Relational Needs—The focus here is on helping people develop authentic, Christ-centered relationships with others. Those who take an interest in meeting these needs find fulfillment in connecting people—helping them find and build satisfying relationships. Those who are drawn to meet such needs tend to use gifts of encouragement, wisdom, hospitality, mercy, discernment, and pastoring.

Emotional Needs—Individuals who are hurting emotionally need reassurance to know who they are in Christ. People who feel gratified by meeting emotional needs tend to be interested in counseling, encouraging and listening to others so that they can help those in pain go through their life situations with Christ. The gifts people use to meet these needs include encouragement, wisdom, mercy, discernment, and pastoring.

Educational Needs—People drawn to minister in this area enjoy everything from helping people learn to showing them how to live life to its fullest. People who have a heart for meeting educational needs tend to enjoy teaching—using a variety of settings, teaching tools, and styles—to stimulate growth. Spiritual gifts expressed here are teaching, pastoring, knowledge, and prophecy.

Vocational Needs—Whether young mothers or Fortune 500 executives, some individuals need help to maximize their personal or professional potential. People who love to meet these needs typically use their expertise to train, coach, and consult with others to overcome barriers and reach goals. The gifts expressed in meeting vocational needs are wisdom, leadership, teaching, encouragement, and discernment.

Ask yourself:

- What are the top two needs I love meeting?
- Why do I love meeting these needs?
- What lessons have I learned that I could pass on to others?

What Cause Will You Help Conquer?

Searching for a way to make a lasting contribution in life, Millard Fuller left behind a trail of business achievements to water a seed God had planted in his heart – building homes for families with little or no income. In the mid 1970s Fuller and a group of associates created a new organization called Habitat for Humanity International. Thirty years later, Habitat has provided basic housing for thousands upon thousands of low-income families and has become one of the most well known community service successes both in the United States and worldwide – all because one ordinary man decided to use what God had given him to champion a cause greater than himself.

Maybe you aren't sensing a personal hunger to help the homeless as Millard Fuller has done, or you may not long to serve people affected by HIV/AIDS as Kay Warren does. But if you live your life with God long enough, he will stir your heart and direct you to the cause he has personally chosen you to take on.

Here is a short list of causes that others have committed to championing for God's glory:

Abortion	Ethics
Abuse/violence	Financial stewardship
Alcoholism	Health and/or fitness
At-risk children	HIV/AIDS
Christ-centered parenting	Homelessness
Compulsive behavior issues	Law and/or justice system
Deafness	Marriage/family issues
Disabilities and/or support	Policy and/or politics
Divorce	Poverty/hunger
Drug abuse/recovery	Sanctity of life
Educational issues	Sexuality and/or gender issues
Environment	Spiritual apathy

Ask yourself:

- What cause or issue makes my heart race?
- Where could I make the greatest impact for God?
- If time wasn't an issue, to what cause would I donate myself?

What Dream Will You Fulfill?

Brandon Ebel is the firstborn son of a prominent senior pastor in the Pacific Northwest. His relationship with Christ began early, as did his passion for music. His parents routinely had to lecture little Brandon about not touching home theater and audio systems when visiting neighbors' homes. One thing was certain: Brandon's love for music would ultimately form the foundation for his Kingdom Purpose.

His musical passion grew throughout college, and he graduated with a bachelor's degree in broadcast communications that landed him a position with a small record label in Southern California. He discovered a knack for business, and soon saw the potential for combining his love for music with his natural business sense.

Brandon had never felt specifically called to serve God as a full-time vocational pastor, but he *did* want to be used by God in a unique and powerful way. Presenting his gifts and passion for music to the Lord, Brandon dreamed of starting his own record label. Now, more than thirteen years later, Tooth and Nail Records and BEC Recordings stand as a benchmark record label in the world of Christian music, all for God's glory.

Brandon didn't sit on the sidelines waiting for God; he took what he had and gave it to God to multiply, just as Jesus did with the bread and fish: "Taking the five loaves and the two fish and looking up to heaven, he gave thanks and broke the loaves. Then he gave them to his disciples to set before the people. He also divided the two fish among them all. They all ate and were satisfied, and the disciples picked up twelve basketfuls of broken pieces of bread and fish. The number of the men who had eaten was five thousand" (Mark 6:41–44; for full context begin at verse 35).

This story always inspires me because it reminds me of how much God wants to bless us and expand our influence for him. God longs to use what he has given us for his glory. He is waiting for us to come to him with thankful hearts and expectant faith. If you were to talk with Brandon today, he would say he is living a great adventure with God, and that it is all *for* God.

In his *Wild at Heart – Field Manual,* John Eldredge says, "Our goal here is to recover that adventure God wrote on your heart when he made you. Your deepest desires reveal your deepest calling, the adventure God has for you. You must decide whether or not you'll exchange a life of control born out of fear for a life of risk born out of faith."

Eldredge continues, "So, if you had permission to do what you really want to do, what would you do? Just start making a list of all the things you deeply desire to do with your life, great and small. And remember – *'Don't ask yourself, How?' How?* is never the right question; *how?* is a faithless question. *How?* is God's department. He is asking you *what?* What is written on your heart? What makes you come alive? If you could do what you've always wanted to do, what would it be?"

Sometimes dreams get buried by jobs that are unfulfilling, situations that are unraveling, "to do" lists that are unending, and finances that are overwhelming. When our attention is on all of the "stuff" in life, our dreams get stifled.

Of course, not every dream that dances in your heart reflects God's will for you. Romans 7 – 8 tell us that the desires of our flesh wage war against the desires of God. Even the apostle Paul admits his personal struggle with this: "I don't understand myself at all, for I really want to do what is right, but I don't do it. Instead, I do the very thing I hate. I know perfectly well that what I am doing is wrong, and my bad conscience shows that I agree that the law is good. But I can't help myself, because it is sin inside me that makes me do these evil things" (Romans 7:15 – 17, NLT).

Sometimes a desire for personal comfort, success, and glory displaces a passion for God's glory. Victory over our selfish desires comes only when the Spirit guides our life. Paul points to this when he says, "For the power of the life-giving Spirit has freed you through Christ Jesus from the power of sin that leads to death" (Romans 8:2, NLT). So yes, dream big – but make sure your dreams align with God's Word and advance his purposes.

Ask yourself:

- What pursuit would release the passion in my life for God?
- What God-centered dreams can I identify that have been buried by life?
- What would I attempt to do for God with the rest of my life?

Connecting with your God-given passions transforms your everyday life. Passions make work seem like play. And our gifts and passions ignite like spiritual rocket fuel, propelling us to new heights of service, when we mix them with our natural abilities.

What do you naturally excel at? In the next chapter, we'll see how your unique abilities play a role in your life being transformed for God. You'll discover how they bring greater color and clarity to the master-piece you are.

GRABBING HOLD

Reflect on what you have learned. What did this chapter show you about your emotional heartbeat?

Realize what you have been given. Paint a word portrait of the emotional heartbeat God has given you.

Request help from others. What two sources of wisdom, support, and encouragement can affirm what you have discovered about yourself or help you further clarify your findings?

Respond in faith. Identify two action steps you can take in the next month to let your heart beat for God.

1. _____

_____

2. _____

_____

Chapter 4

ABILITIES

Discovering What You Are Naturally Good At

God has given each of us the ability
to do certain things well.
Romans 12:6a (NLT)

Show me a person who doesn't know his talents
or hasn't developed them for service to others,
and I will show you a person who has little sense
of purpose, meaning, motivation and value.
Tom Paterson

God has given you incredible strengths.

My wife stared at me from across our kitchen island. I knew she expected me to say something in reply to what she had just unloaded. I prayed for the right words.

"I'm just a mom," she'd said. "I really don't have much to offer at this season of my life, Erik. All I do is clean, cook, and shuttle kids from one activity to another. It is a twenty-four-hour-a-day, seven-day-a-week assignment. There's little time to rest and less time to think about fulfilling my special purpose from God."

It was the end of a busy day—and she was nearing the end of her rope. By now I knew she didn't need a strategic plan from me; what she needed and wanted was a sensitive ear and heart.

We took a piece of paper and wrote down ten things she loved to do: coach, inspire, run, counsel, encourage, listen, help, read, provide, and organize.

Then we looked at her current commitments, to see where these awesome abilities could be put to use for God at this time in her life. Every morning at 5:30 she exercised with a group of women—a perfect opportunity to coach, inspire, and encourage others. Then there were the women in our small group at church. They needed her gifts too. Her ability to organize and help could be used to orchestrate the annual pastors' wives retreat and quarterly gatherings.

By evening's end, she'd begun to see that God could use her natural abilities during any and every season of her life. All she needed was to be available and aware. It didn't matter whether what she did was noticed by others. That is never the point of serving God. Willing hearts are his delight.

The point isn't whether what she's doing right now is her ultimate Kingdom Purpose, which it very well could be. The truth is, motherhood is a *big* deal.

But my wife, like many women today, simply wanted to do more for God. By making these little deposits of love into others' lives, she is paying into her account for God. As someone once profoundly stated, "The difference between an ordinary day and an extraordinary day is not so much what you do, but who you do it for."

Maybe this season in your life doesn't include being a parent, but you're still wondering how you can use your natural God-given abilities to bring glory to his name. More often than not, we enjoy doing the things we do well. Rick Warren writes: "The abilities you *do* have are a strong indication of what God wants you to do with your life. They are clues to knowing God's will for you.... God doesn't waste abilities; he matches our calling and our capabilities."

Take a few moments to think about what you love doing, the tasks you feel confident performing. This review will help you discover the specific ways you can make deposits of love through serving. God wants one fact to hit home with us: he "has given each of us the ability to do certain things well" (Romans 12:6a, NLT). Like my wife and millions of others, you too excel at doing certain things.

Throughout your life, you discover things you naturally love to do. That also means there are certain things you can live *without* doing. The things you enjoy doing make work more like play. When opportunities to do those things arise, they trigger an energized anticipation to get started. It doesn't seem tiring or time-consuming. People in your life may even comment that what you do seems effortless because of the ease and the sense of joy that's evident when you do it.

This joy and ease can be translated into how you use your abilities for the sake of others. In her book, *Discovering Your Divine Assignment*, Robin Chaddock asks, "Have you ever had someone say to you 'Thank you so much' and your response was 'But I didn't do anything'? ... People will be healed by God through you just being and doing what God meant you to be and do, not by all the things you think you should be and do to benefit the world."

So the question to ask yourself is, "Where do I naturally excel?" Are you someone who loves to inspire others? Do you find yourself frequently delivering a "can-do" message? Is creative thinking just part of how you do things? Do you love to work with your hands? Are you musically talented? Are you known as a team builder? Is goal-setting a natural part of your life? Do you regularly set and meet objectives? Are you excited by the challenge of refreshing and improving programs? Do you have a track record of vision casting and getting people excited about the direction of the vision? Whatever you are naturally good at and love to do—find a way to use it for God!

Maybe you already are using your natural abilities for God. If so, God bless you! But have you considered that God may have more for you? Do you long for something more? God may be saying, "Stretch, beloved! Grow!"

For years, Peggy thought she was following God's purpose for her life. Trained as a writer and editor, she saw her job as a corporate newsletter editor as a way to use her gifts and the people around her as her mission field. But gradually she sensed there should be something else. One day she picked up Bob Briner's book, *Roaring Lambs*, which encourages Christians to use their abilities to impact the world for Christ.

She knew that message was for her.

"A few years later, my pastor was writing this little book called *The Purpose Driven® Life*," Peggy told me. "That voice inside was getting louder. I found myself on my knees daily, surrendering my life for his use. Before long, I met an author who 'happened' to be writing a book on a topic I was passionate about. 'Perhaps you can help me with it,' the author suggested. Neither one of us had any idea what God had in mind! I went on to become the third member of the team that created the book—a huge life purpose for me. But God had even more in store.

"Because of that connection, I learned about possibilities I never knew existed and recognized God's hand at work. Today I'm using my gifts, passions, and abilities to help others maximize their moment for God through writing. I believe that pleases God—to see his children helping each other."

God never finishes showing us his purpose—as long as we never stop seeking it. We are made to be used by God.

In *Shaped by God*, Max Lucado shows how not being put to use leads to loss of purpose:

> To find me, look over in the corner of the shop, over here, behind the cobwebs, beneath the dust, in the darkness. There are scores of us, broken handles, dulled blades, cracked iron. Some of us were useful once, and then ... many of us never were. But, listen, don't feel sorry

for me. Life ain't so bad here in the pile … no work, no anvils, no pain, no sharpening. And yet, the days are very long.

The days *would* be very long – *life* would be very long and dull – without the expectant hope of being used for a purpose greater than ourselves.

As you think about your particular strengths and areas of interest, the idea is not meant to boost your self-esteem by pointing out how qualified you are. Rather it is to remind us how exceedingly qualified God is to put into action anything he created. Our strengths and abilities show off *his* greatness and magnitude.

As a pastor, I have seen many people struggle with identifying their natural abilities. They have lost focus on what they love doing and where they excel. All too often we become so focused on doing only what we think we should do – or feel pressure to continue doing – in order to pay for a certain lifestyle. We discover freedom from these pressures when we pursue the activities for which God has uniquely designed us. Which life do you want?

In Charles Dickens's classic story, *A Christmas Carol*, the cash-obsessed Ebenezer Scrooge encounters the ghost of his deceased business partner, Jacob Marley. Scrooge compliments Marley on his exceptional business savvy. Marley's selfishness in life, however, condemned him to observe in death those things he could have changed if he had only been willing. He snaps at Scrooge's selfish comment: "Business! Mankind was my business. The common welfare was my business; charity, mercy, forbearance and benevolence were all my business. The dealings of my trade were but a drop of water in the comprehensive ocean of my business!"

Jacob Marley learned too late that his strengths and abilities were wasted by his own dogged determination to live for nothing but money. In life, he'd convinced himself that what was "good for business" was his most important purpose. Now, in death, he warned Scrooge about being enslaved to the same mentality.

Have you, like Scrooge, lost your focus? Are you distracted by self-serving values? I encourage you to reevaluate the abilities God has given you in light of his eternal purposes and the life situation in which he has placed you. What you discover could set you free – and open the door to a fulfilling ministry you've never even imagined!

Embrace the Things You Love to Do

On pages 74 and 75, you'll find a list of fifty specialized abilities. As you review each one, you will be asked to indicate whether you love it, like it, or could live without it. The goal is for you to embrace the things you *love* to do, not just the things you *can* do. Your job, for example, may require you to lead. But you may not have a genuine desire for leading. If that is the case, why include leadership as part of your unique S.H.A.P.E.?

It's easy to forget this in our day-after-day life, but one day each one of us will give an account to God for what we did with the talents he gave us—so make the most of your talents now! Life is too short to settle for less than doing our best for God. Arthur F. Miller Jr. writes: "Understand that you are God's idea. You will be held accountable for using what he gave you to work with."

When Annie became aware of a youth ministry opportunity at church in which her specific abilities could help others worship God, she served from a desire to be obedient. Although she felt joy in that ministry, she realized she was not serving in her unique "Sweet Spot."

While working with the high school students, Annie learned that many of them longed to worship God through art, but had no opportunity. She began searching for a way to use her own artistic ability, realizing she had a responsibility to use the talent God had created within her. As she began her art ministry, Annie found she had been blessed to be a blessing to others. She helped young adults display their love and awe for God in new and even unconventional ways.

Worshiping God should never be conventional or contrived, but it's much too easy to fall into what's familiar. All too often, we limit ourselves to a few habits. Annie saw an opportunity to change that for the high school students God had put right in front of her.

Annie's experience shows how important it is to identify and embrace our God-given abilities. I love how she says it: "I could be doing art anywhere, but I have found much more fulfillment and meaning in doing it for God." Annie surrendered both her abilities and passions to God, and she found a purpose that changed other lives.

The great nineteenth-century preacher Andrew Murray made this analogy: "I have a pen in my pocket that is surrendered to its purpose of writing and must be surrendered to my hand if I am to write with it properly. If someone has a partial hold on it, I cannot write with it." By the same token, if we hold back the natural abilities God gave us at birth – or if we use those abilities for purposes that don't include God – those talents will not be used to their full capacity.

Do you know what abilities you were born with? If not, your answers to the following questions should help. As you review each ability, rank yourself according to whether you love it, like it, or can live without it.

Love It!

You can't imagine life without these activities. They make your day complete. Given a choice, you would do these things full-time. These abilities are the way you will meet the needs of the people group you identified in the last chapter. They can be – but don't have to be – part of your job. Your nine-to-five life may be just tent-making, as it was for the apostle Paul. If you are unsatisfied by what you do full-time, finding what you love to do most could become what you do full-time.

Like It!

You may enjoy these activities, but don't need to do them on a regular basis in order to feel satisfied. Your attitude toward them is "I can take it or leave it." For example, you may enjoy coaching or teaching, but these things don't satisfy you like the things you really love.

Live Without!

These activities leave you feeling slightly deflated and disappointed, compared to what you love doing. When faced with the prospect of having to do these things, your immediate response is to think about *not* doing them. When you have to carry out these responsibilities on a frequent basis, you feel drained. You may be able to adequately perform these tasks, but you have little or no desire to do them.

Fifty Specialized Abilities

The following abilities are fairly common, but this alphabetical list is in no way exhaustive. All abilities matter to God. In his eyes, all are equally

important. If your particular ability isn't listed, be sure to note it on your
S.H.A.P.E. *for* Life Profile in Appendix 1 on pages 221–223.

Check the natural abilities you excel at and "love" doing.

☐ **Adapting**: The ability to adjust, change, alter, modify.

☐ **Administrating**: The ability to govern, run, rule.

☐ **Analyzing**: The ability to examine, investigate, probe, evaluate.

☐ **Building**: The ability to construct, make, assemble.

☐ **Coaching**: The ability to prepare, instruct, train, equip, develop.

☐ **Communicating**: The ability to share, convey, impart.

☐ **Competing**: The ability to contend, win, battle.

☐ **Computing**: The ability to add, estimate, total, calculate.

☐ **Connecting**: The ability to link together, involve, relate.

☐ **Consulting**: The ability to advise, discuss, confer.

☐ **Cooking**: The ability to prepare, serve, feed, cater.

☐ **Coordinating**: The ability to organize, match, harmonize.

☐ **Counseling**: The ability to guide, advise, support, listen, care for.

☐ **Decorating**: The ability to beautify, enhance, adorn.

☐ **Designing**: The ability to draw, create, picture, outline.

☐ **Developing**: The ability to expand, grow, advance, increase.

☐ **Directing**: The ability to aim, oversee, manage, supervise.

☐ **Editing**: The ability to correct, amend, alter, improve.

☐ **Encouraging**: The ability to cheer, inspire, support.

☐ **Engineering**: The ability to construct, design, plan.

☐ **Facilitating**: The ability to help, aid, assist, make possible.

☐ **Forecasting**: The ability to predict, calculate, see trends, patterns, and themes.

☐ **Implementing**: The ability to apply, execute, make happen.

☐ **Improving**: The ability to better, enhance, further, enrich.

☐ **Influencing**: The ability to affect, sway, shape, change.

☐ **Landscaping**: The ability to garden, plant, improve.

☐ **Leading**: The ability to pave the way, direct, excel, win.

☐ **Learning**: The ability to study, gather, understand, improve, expand self.

☐ **Managing**: The ability to run, handle, oversee.

☐ **Mentoring**: The ability to advise, guide, teach.

☐ **Motivating**: The ability to provoke, induce, prompt.

☐ **Negotiating**: The ability to discuss, consult, settle.

☐ **Operating**: The ability to run mechanical or technical things.

☐ **Organizing**: The ability to simplify, arrange, fix, classify, coordinate.

☐ **Performing**: The ability to sing, speak, dance, play an instrument, act out.

☐ **Pioneering**: The ability to bring about something new, groundbreaking, original.

☐ **Planning**: The ability to arrange, map out, prepare.

☐ **Promoting**: The ability to sell, sponsor, endorse, showcase.

☐ **Recruiting**: The ability to draft, enlist, hire, engage.

☐ **Repairing**: The ability to fix, mend, restore, heal.

☐ **Researching**: The ability to seek, gather, examine, study.

☐ **Resourcing**: The ability to furnish, provide, deliver.

☐ **Serving**: The ability to help, assist, fulfill.

☐ **Strategizing**: The ability to think ahead, calculate, scheme.

☐ **Teaching**: The ability to explain, demonstrate, tutor.

☐ **Translating**: The ability to interpret, decode, explain, speak.

☐ **Traveling**: The ability to journey, visit, explore.

☐ **Visualizing**: The ability to picture, imagine, envision, dream, conceptualize.

☐ **Welcoming**: The ability to entertain, greet, embrace, make comfortable.

☐ **Writing**: The ability to compose, create, record.

Your top abilities: Assuming that you've checked more than five of the fifty items, go back and choose the five that most define you. If you've chosen five or less, note them here also.

1. _____

2. _____

3. _____

4. _____

5. _____

Now transfer these to your S.H.A.P.E. *for* Life Profile in Appendix 1 on pages 221–223.

Expressing What You Love to Do

Look once more at your list of top abilities. Is there anything on that list you couldn't live without? Remember, the goal is to embrace and express the natural abilities – those things God has allowed you to excel at – so you can use them to fulfill your Kingdom Purpose without anxiety or fear of failure.

Michelangelo said, "The greater danger for most of us is not that our aim is too high and we miss it, but that it is too low and we reach it." We ought to live our lives waiting to hear God say, "Well done!"

Remember how my wife, Stacey, made the list of ten things she loved to do? You have just made a list like that for yourself! Now do what Stacey did next: Think of some small things you can do for others every day to naturally express your love and heart to serve.

• What are some ways you can use the things you love to do to make little deposits of love *in your home* this next week?

• What are some ways you can use the things you love to do to make little deposits of love *at work* this next week?

• What are some ways you can use the things you love to do to make little deposits of love *at church* this next week?

• What are some ways you can use the things you love to do to make little deposits of love *in your small group* this next week?

Have you ever heard of a guy named Shamgar? I confess he wasn't on top of my Bible character list either, until I read a book about him, *The Three Success Secrets of Shamgar*, by Pat Williams, Jay Strack, and Jim Denney.

Shamgar was one of the Hebrew judges, who lived between the time of Joshua and King Saul. Shamgar didn't get a lot of space in the Bible, but what he did was huge. Outnumbered six hundred to one by an army of Philistines, Shamgar used an oxgoad to kill all of them (see Judges 3:31). What was so special about Shamgar?

"Shamgar was just an average person, no different from ... you," writes Pat Williams. "He was an ordinary human being who lived in extraordinary times, just as we do today.... Fact is, if you aren't willing to take on six-hundred-to-one odds, you'll never achieve anything great. Nothing worth doing is ever easy. Significant achievements always involve a high degree of courage, focus, perseverance, and yes, risk."

Jay Strack then recalls the night when he, a young man who'd known a lifetime of abuse, heard evangelist E. V. Hill tell Shamgar's story: "[Hill] was one of the most powerful preachers I have ever heard. I can still hear his voice ringing in my memory: 'Shamgar did what he could, with what he had, right where he was—and every chance he got.'"

The point is, if you're willing to risk it all by giving your abilities to God, you too can overcome six-hundred-to-one odds. Statistically, I shouldn't be a pastor today. Experts tell us abused kids are most likely to never become productive citizens. The prisons are full of proof. But I was abused, and once I put all that I am in God's hands, he helped me overcome odds that were at least six hundred to one.

In his essay, "The Weight of Glory," C. S. Lewis writes: "It would seem that our Lord finds our desires not too strong, but too weak. We are half-hearted creatures, fooling about with drink and sex and ambition when infinite joy is offered us, like an ignorant child who wants to go on making mud pies in a slum because he cannot imagine what is meant by the offer of a holiday at the sea. We are far too easily pleased."

Whatever God is showing you in these pages about your unique life purpose, I urge you not to go about it halfheartedly. Stretch for the infinite joy. Dare to be a Shamgar!

One way to do that is to let your abilities shine through the unique personality God gave you. It's tempting to want to be like someone else, but that's cheating God, yourself—and others. God has a distinct mission that can only be accomplished by *you being you.*

GRABBING HOLD

Reflect on what you have learned. What have you learned about God and how he wants you to apply your abilities?

Realize what you have been given. Write God a thank-you note for the natural abilities he has graced you with.

Request help from others. What two people can you connect with this week to review the things you love to do? This feedback will help you determine whether or not your motives are all about giving and not getting.

Respond in faith. Identify two action steps you can take in the next month to better express what you love to do.

1. _____

_____

2. _____

_____

Chapter 5

PERSONALITY

Discovering Who God Made You to Be

Like stained glass, our different personalities
reflect God's light in many colors and patterns.
Rick Warren

The art of being yourself at your best is the art of unfolding
your personality into the person you want to be....
Be gentle with yourself, learn to love yourself, to forgive yourself,
for only as we have the right attitude toward ourselves
can we have the right attitude toward others.
Wilfred Peterson

Embrace the person God made you to be.

"My personality style is not one that is going to make me very visible. Does that mean I'm less valuable?"

Shelly used to think that the people who are outgoing and competitive are the ones used most by God. When she compared herself to their football-player-like aggressiveness, she felt inadequate for God's purposes.

God, however, doesn't measure people the way most of us do. While the world places value on externals like prestige, position, and wealth, God places the highest value on less visible aspects of our lives.

Eventually Shelly realized that the personality God had given her reflected qualities custom-designed by her Creator so she could fulfill a unique and valuable Kingdom Purpose. For years she has worked as an editor for various authors, which has resulted in helping readers better understand the author's message. Although the way she uses her talents and gifts keeps her behind the scenes rather than on the cover, in God's eyes she has no less star power than the authors themselves.

Just as the Lord gave you unique spiritual gifts, passions, and abilities, the personality you have also is his gift to you. He created it and gave it to you to use for his glory.

In an effort to explain the differences in human personalities, experts have created many different methods of categorizing personality traits. Authors Gary Smalley and John Trent, for example, use animal names such as Beaver, Otter, Retriever, and Lion to explain how these animals' traits reflect our own personalities. Popular speaker and author Florence Littauer uses the words _popular, powerful, perfect_, and _peaceful_ to represent various personal styles.

Psychologists also have developed various tests to identify and categorize specific personality behaviors. Arthur F. Miller Jr. explains that these kinds of tests can be limiting and much too generalized: "[The] highness or the lowness of a score is not a measurement of an individual's worth or value. Each person functions in a unique way. Traits have been separated out from the vast complexity of human functioning as a convenience to us."

Rick Warren uses four traditional temperament styles – sanguine, choleric, melancholy, and phlegmatic – to talk about personality:

> The Bible gives us plenty of evidence for the fact that God uses all types of personalities. Peter was a *sanguine*. Paul was a *choleric*. Jeremiah was a *melancholy*. If you take a closer look at the personality differences in the twelve disciples, it's easy to see why they sometimes had interpersonal conflict.
>
> There is no "right" or "wrong" temperament for ministry. We need all kinds of personalities to balance the church and give it flavor. The world would be a very boring place if we were all plain vanilla. Fortunately, people come in more than thirty-one flavors.

As you can see, there is more than one way to slice and dice the individual personality. The one constant is this indisputable truth: *God has instilled a unique personality in each one of us for his glory.*

This chapter is designed to help you embrace this truth. Understanding the personality God has given you will help you more effectively express your spiritual gifts, heart, and abilities for his sake.

In order to help you better understand your personality, we will consider two things:

1. *How you relate to others*: Your Kingdom Purpose is all about people, so it is important to discover how you relate to others.
2. *How you respond to opportunities*: You will encounter many serving opportunities throughout your life, so understanding how you react to various situations will help you make the best choices.

By looking at these "how's," you will gain a better understanding of the personality characteristics with which God has graced you. Webster defines personality as "the complex of characteristics that distinguishes an individual." These characteristics affect the way you think, the way you feel, and the way you act. Your personality characteristics influence your entire life – from decision making to dealing with change, from solving problems to resolving conflict, from engaging people to expressing feelings, from competing to cooperating. Your personality takes center stage in all areas of your life!

People simply are different from one another. Authors Jane A. G. Kise, David Stark, and Sandra Krebs Hirsh put it this way in their book, *LifeKeys: Discovering Who You Are, Why You're Here, What You Do Best*:

> These differences are natural, God-given aspects of personality. Being who you are — the person God intended you to be — is of paramount importance ... the differences make life interesting. Can you imagine what the world would be like if everyone were just like you — your gifts and your shortcomings magnified by the billions?

At one time or another, don't we all think the world might be just a little bit better/easier/more satisfying "if only" more people were like us? The unspoken desire behind that thought is for other people to adhere to our expectations. None of us has that option, and it's obvious God never planned it that way. One look at the world around us makes it clear that God loves variety — even if we're not personally very fond of some of it!

God didn't create other people to please you — and he didn't create you to please them. He made us to please him. He created all of us to relate differently, feel differently, react differently, and respond to life differently. Though our culture often portrays outgoing and unreserved people as the model of "success," such a view is misleading and harmful. We do not have to conform to the expectations of others in order to feel we have accomplished something worthwhile in life.

In *Why You Can't Be Anything You Want to Be*, Arthur F. Miller Jr. says:

> Perhaps you are unaware of the fact that you are the customized expression of a loving God. You have been endowed with a unique mix of competencies and the desire and drive to use them in pursuit of an outcome of unrivaled personal importance. Your life has meaning built into it. Effectively, you have an exciting, challenging, and achievable destiny if you will but discover and embrace who you were designed to be.

God gave you a unique personality. He did it intentionally as part of his process of creating the masterpiece of your life. Allow him, then, to help you understand your personality so you can bring him the greatest glory possible.

Relating to Others

Have you ever walked into a room full of complete strangers? How did you react? Some people see an opportunity to meet and mingle with new people, while others look for a place to hide! Do you realize that the impulse to mingle is not necessarily better than the inclination to hide? Those are just two ways that different people respond to the same situation.

During the course of my ministry, I have noticed that when it comes to relating to others, people's responses tend to fall into certain categories. Let's look at a few clues about your relationship style and how it lines up with God's desire for you.

Outgoing or Reserved?

If you prefer interacting with many people and tend to gain energy from being around them, then God may have wired you to be outgoing. On the other hand, if you prefer interacting with just a few people at a time—or maybe even one-on-one—and you find your energy renewed through quiet, reflective time, then your nature is more reserved. Personally, I'm somewhere in the middle. I like to be around people and enjoy their company, but I am more energized by being alone for times of reflection and solitude.

Which of these statements best describes you? *I tend to ...*

- Look for ways to be part of the crowd.
- Build deep relationships with a few individuals, as opposed to many people.
- Start conversations with people I don't know.
- Hesitate in being part of a large group.

Self-expressive or Self-controlled?

If you tend to be open and verbal with your thoughts and opinions and enjoy sharing them with others, you would be considered self-expressive. By contrast, if you tend to keep your thoughts and opinions to yourself, you may be described as self-controlled.

My buddy Jeff is very outgoing. But when it comes to sharing his life with people, he is definitely self-controlled. Before he will show his emotions to others, Jeff must build a deep level of trust. I have another friend, however, who seldom hesitates to tell you how he is feeling, even if he just met you. He has no problem expressing his feelings and thoughts to many people – as long as they're willing to listen.

Again, identify your tendencies. *I tend to* ...

- Share my feelings freely with those I have just met.
- Withhold my thoughts and feelings from others at certain times.
- Seek opportunities to share my life with others.
- Hold my cards closer to my chest so that only a few individuals can *truly* know me.

Cooperative or Competitive?

Do you commonly accept the opinions of others without disagreement? Is it your aim in life to resist conflict as much as possible, attempting to live peacefully with others at all times? If so, you are likely to be more cooperative in relating to others. However, if you enjoy winning and over-coming obstacles, and if you love to embrace challenges, you would be considered more competitive in nature. We all know people who don't have a competitive bone in their body – and others who have the competitive intensity of a professional athlete!

What about you? *I tend to* ...

- Focus on making sure people are okay when I'm around them.
- Find importance in achievements.
- Embrace conflict and enjoy winning.
- Look for ways to make others content.

There is nothing unusual about being a combination of different personality tendencies. God is not limited to working within some psychologist's list of traits. In fact, he wants us to avoid being pigeonholed or labeled – either by others or by ourselves.

Relating Recap

So how would you describe the way you relate to others based on the categories we just looked at? Personally, I tend to be more reserved, self-controlled, and very competitive. What about you? Circle the words below that BEST describe the way you relate to others. You can circle the "x" in the middle if your personality style includes both traits.

Outgoing	X	Reserved
Self-expressive	X	Self-controlled
Cooperative	X	Competitive

Your Response to Opportunities

If you had the opportunity to choose the ideal situation that would enable you to make the greatest difference for God, what would it look like? You may find it helpful to think back over the past year or so of your life and survey the opportunities that brought you the greatest fulfillment and yielded the best results. Like a farmer surveying his fall harvest, which opportunities produced the most "fruit"?

Take a look at the following categories, designed to help you understand the way you react when God brings you an opportunity.

High Risk or Low Risk?

Some of us seek out situations that involve risks, while others avoid risks at all costs and, if presented with uncertain circumstances, we run as far from them as possible. Do you naturally gravitate toward opportunities for serving that involve few risks with few changes, or does your heart race with adrenaline when opportunities arise that come with a higher level of risk attached to them?

Consider your own comfort zones. *I tend to ...*

- Avoid too much change.
- Relish chaotic environments.
- Thrive when risk is very low.
- Become motivated when I have the chance to overcome obstacles in order to achieve success.

People or Projects?

My friend Dawn loves people. All of them. She would sign up for any opportunity that involved people. While Dawn is efficient in completing projects, she tends to be more people-oriented than process- and project-oriented. What about you? Do you get excited about opportunities that involve people or do you prefer situations that require behind-the-scenes work on projects that help people?

I tend to ...

- Embrace opportunities that impact people directly.
- Look for ways to complete projects.
- Enjoy orchestrating and coordinating many projects.
- Find fulfillment when I am able to work with someone one-on-one or in a small group.

Follow or Lead?

The personalities of Jesus' twelve closest disciples certainly reflect variety. There was a hard-nosed tax collector and a couple of political activists. There was Andrew, a behind-the-scenes sort, and his brother, Simon, a bull-in-a-china-shop, take-charge kind of guy. You may be willing to follow the leadership of others, like Andrew, or perhaps you flourish when you are the one leading. Again, there are no right or wrong temperaments. It is simply a matter of understanding how God created you.

I tend to ...

- Find myself in positions of leadership.
- Feel comfortable when I can follow someone else.
- Impact others with my life.
- Receive fulfillment by helping others find success.

Team or Solo?

Some people naturally gravitate toward opportunities that include working with a team, while others feel they can make a stronger impact by working alone or with a small number of people. Do you feel that being part of a team is important for a successful outcome? Or do you believe you have greater impact on your own?

I tend to ...

- Enjoy working within a team environment.
- Look for opportunities that allow me to operate solo.

- Become energized by being around others.
- Work most effectively when I'm alone.

Routine or Variety?

If you prefer activities that clearly define what is expected of you, and completion of the activity is within reach, you tend to be more routine in nature. If, on the other hand, you enjoy involvement with many projects, that's a good indication that variety will be part of your unique Kingdom Purpose.

I tend to ...

- Begin many projects at one time.
- Find fulfillment when I can complete one project at a time.
- Have a high capacity and look for ways to spin many plates.
- Become overwhelmed with constant change.

Responding Recap

So how do you respond to opportunities when they present themselves? I typically prefer opportunities that involve moderate risk, projects that impact people, leading, working with small teams, and lots of variety. What makes a day fulfilling for you? Circle the words below that BEST describe the way you respond to opportunities to contribute. Again, you may circle the "x" in the middle if your personality style borders both traits.

High-risk	X	Low-risk
People	X	Process / Projects
Follow	X	Lead
Teamwork	X	Solo
Routine	X	Variety

Be True to Who God Made You to Be

It will be hard to fulfill your Kingdom Purpose if you take on ministry opportunities that don't align with the way God has fashioned you. Too often people settle for good opportunities when they could be embracing great ones for God. If you are more cooperative, don't try to be competitive. If you are naturally reserved, don't try to force yourself to be more outgoing. If you enjoy routine, don't take on things that are constantly changing.

Attempting to conform to personality types and patterns that are outside our natural S.H.A.P.E. goes against everything God, as our Creator, wants us to grasp about ourselves. We honor God when we accept our distinct personalities and use them for his purposes; not just accept them grudgingly—with an "if I have to" attitude—but joyfully live out the S.H.A.P.E. God created within us.

Of course, each of us can work outside our personality pattern for a while. You can choose to use (or not use) your personality any way you'd like. In fact, sometimes we need to venture out in order to discover our full personality. But if you continually stay outside your own personality style—trying to be someone you're not—you will be ineffective for God. There are no wrong people in life; only the right people doing the wrong things.

I have seen this mistake played out in the careers of many people who have been asked to find new territory when they truly desire to "mind the camp." The mismatch has caused these individuals to come to a point of total frustration with their jobs. God did not create you to live in a state of frustration or discouragement; he intended you to experience deep fulfillment that only comes from being who he made you to be.

Lory's high-powered career made good use of her abilities and talents, but the male-dominated work environment was not a good fit for her personality. Lory forced herself to adapt—she had a lot to contribute, and using her abilities gave her a sense of gratification—but she was missing a deeper sense of fulfillment. She needed a way to express the part of her personality that longed to serve others. As Lory puts it, "I felt unfinished."

Instead of finding a new job somewhere else, Lory chose to take early retirement and plunged headlong into serving others at church through her S.H.A.P.E. Now her daily life shows God's handiwork and brings Lory the kind of fulfillment that only expressing her true personality can bring.

If your present workplace is having a negative affect on your spirit, consider the possibility that God is using the situation as a test. I have found that God always wants to do something "in us" before he wants to do something "through us." So he may want you to stay until you learn to accept with humility his plans and purposes for you. But you also ought to know that you don't have to stay in a frustrating place when God has something better in mind for you. There are several things you can do to bring your personality to the forefront of your daily work:

Talk with your boss. Perhaps you could ask your boss if you can take on other responsibilities that better align with your personality and S.H.A.P.E. Tell him or her what you feel more fulfilled doing and point out that those activities result in more effective overall performance for the company. When I worked in the corporate world, I took such a risk and it paid off. Go in open-handed and just share with your supervisor where you feel you can help make a larger impact for the company.

Find a better match. (Consider finding a position that allows you to express a higher percentage of who God has made you to be. I always encourage people to shoot for an 80/20 split, which means spending 80 percent of your time working on objectives that fully embrace how God has wired you, and 20 percent on objectives that just need to be done.)

Reduce your expenses. Perhaps you are in your current job simply because it provides an income for you. Can you strategize a way to reduce your expenses in order to begin faithfully living as the person you were meant to be, with the personality you were meant to live out? Many people try to serve two masters, which the Bible says is impossible. Your life will either be guided by the Master or by money. Don't fall prey to this trap of Satan's. Finding a way to live more simply may give you the freedom to find a job that's better aligned with your personality and S.H.A.P.E. Be wise with your resources and, in turn, increase your effectiveness for God.

Ask for help. Don't journey into a transition alone. Ask your friends and your family members—the people who know you best—how they see your personality and S.H.A.P.E. being expressed in a particular career. Ask them how they see you using your personality to make a significant contribution with your life. Ask God to help you find the doors that lead you to fulfillment.

Start volunteering. Look for opportunities to volunteer at your church or within your community that allow you to put your God-given personality and S.H.A.P.E. into action. There are many wonderful churches and community organizations in need of people to simply help. If you attend church, don't just give your money, but your time and talents as well. Saddleback Church would not be where it is today if it were not for the thousands of volunteers who use their S.H.A.P.E. to serve God.

One last thought: Being effective for God through your S.H.A.P.E. does not necessarily mean that you are in the wrong career if you don't yet see God revealing his unique purpose in your life. If it feels like something is missing, perhaps you need to be more faithful with the opportunity God has given you rather than waiting for perfect conditions.

In his groundbreaking book, *Roaring Lambs*, the late Bob Briner reflects on the times when he, a successful sports executive, would find himself asking, "Why am I here?" As a Christian, he'd been led to believe all his life that a person had to be serving in full-time ministry to make a difference. What he discovered was that all believers are called into full-time ministry — but that ministry often is expressed through a career in the marketplace. "What a shame," Briner wrote, "that so many of us feel sort of in a fog between our faith and our careers. I am convinced that many Christians have no idea about the possibility of being lambs that roar — of being followers of God who know how to fully integrate their commitment to Christ into their daily lives. Maybe that's why so many areas of modern life are lacking the preserving salt of the Gospel."

I hope I've made it apparent that God doesn't mean for us to be labeled as a personality "type." I agree with the way the authors of *LifeKeys* put it: "While there are some similarities among people of the same type, type doesn't explain *everything* about you or anyone else. [Type] does, however, do an excellent job of helping you understand yourself, appreciate others, know the work/service setting that is best for you and make sense of some of your life choices."

The personality God created in you is meant to be embraced because it is a reflection of your overall S.H.A.P.E. — the way he made you in order to use you for his glory. God does not create anything that does not have tremendous value and enormous potential — and he will not use anyone who does not have a willing spirit.

Over the course of your life, God has given you experiences that your personality responded to in unique ways. How do you suppose God wants to use the events of your life to help you accomplish the mission he has set aside just for you? Let's explore that question next.

GRABBING HOLD

Reflect on what you have learned. What are a few things you learned about God from this chapter?

Realize what you have been given. Summarize your primary personality pattern below. What is the mix that makes up your unique wiring from God? What types of opportunities will you embrace for God's glory?

Request help from others. Who are two sources of wisdom, support, and encouragement with whom you can share your findings to affirm or help you further clarify what you've discovered about yourself?

Respond in faith. What are two steps you can take in the next month to allow your personality to shine for God's glory?

1. _____

_____

2. _____

_____

Chapter 6

EXPERIENCES

Discovering Where You Have Been

The marvelous richness of human experience
would lose something of rewarding joy
if there were no limitations to overcome.
The hilltop hour would not be so wonderful
if there were not dark valleys to traverse.
Helen Keller

And we know that in all things God works
for the good of those who love him,
who have been called according to his purpose.
Romans 8:28

Life can only be understood backwards,
but it must be lived forwards.
Søren Kierkegaard

There is purpose in your past.

An automobile accident in May 1996 took the life of singer and songwriter Jana Alayra's four-year-old daughter, Lynnie. It was an excruciating loss. "It's every parent's worst nightmare," Jana says. "There were so many tears. I remember reeling and feeling as though I would stumble at any moment. I was reaching out to grab hold of something to stop the downward spiral—and found the hand of our Savior. I threw myself at the foot of the cross and said, 'Lord, you'd better be who you say you are, or there's no point in this life. Lynnie is yours—and so am I.'

"The grace and love of God rushed in, in more ways than I can begin to tell you. Sometimes that comfort came in the words of a friend. Sometimes it was in a Scripture someone pasted to a flower they left on my door. Sometimes it was on a tear-soaked page of my Bible. But I grabbed hold of Jesus. He is the Rock. He is unshakable. He is hope. He is eternal life.

"Now, nearly a decade later, it seems that on a weekly and sometimes daily basis I hear about tragic losses like the kind I experienced. Someone will write or call and ask if there is a word I could share—a CD, a song, anything—with a friend who just lost a child. What a joy to be able to be that word of truth to afflicted moms and dads of all kinds who've said unexpected goodbyes to a child. What an honor to be a conduit of his love—to be his arms of love for hurting parents."

Jana Alayra is a wife, a mother of three young daughters, and a friend. She also is a musical artist who leads worship—in a small group with her guitar, singing for a thousand children and their families. In the mix of these things, Jana is expressing her unique Kingdom Purpose. Her enthusiasm and love for Christ are evident, sincere, and inspiring. You can see it in her character.

Jana made an important decision in her life. She could have turned away from God in bitterness over her loss. Instead, she ran into his arms and allowed her crisis to become a catalyst for Christ. Faith and experience taught her that true comfort is found in God alone. If she let him—because

God always gives us a choice—he would help her through this painful experience in her life. Although many people were by her side through that painful time, God was in the deepest part of her life, healing her wounds and showing her how to turn her pain into gain for him.

Hallway of Life

As God slowly crafts the masterpiece of our lives, he uses all of our experiences—the painful as well as the enjoyable—to flesh out the finished product. Think back over all the key experiences of your life that have shaped who you are today: childhood joys and sorrows, the pain and thrill of adolescence, the struggle and accomplishment of adulthood.

Imagine yourself walking down a long hallway. On the walls are paintings that reflect those life-shaping moments in your life. On one side are portraits of experiences that brought you excitement, achievement, and fulfillment. On the other side hang pictures of experiences that caused pain, frustration, and remorse. Walking slowly down that hallway, looking carefully at each painting, is an important step toward understanding who God has created you to be and discovering the Kingdom Purpose he has set aside just for you.

As you examine each life-event portrait that God brings to mind, take time to think about how it has ultimately impacted you. What lessons did you glean? If you can't think of any lessons, ask God to reveal them to you. He longs to use *everything* in your life. To get the most out of this chapter, seek a breakthrough with God. Be fully transparent. Celebrate your victories and claim your pain for God's gain. Go deep below the surface and think of the earnest moments and significant experiences that truly define your life story.

Positive Portraits

Arthur F. Miller Jr. is one of the world's leading experts in self-development. Many companies use his SIMA® talent coaching program with great success. His work has changed the landscape of today's workplace for everyone from corporate leaders to librarians, from letter carriers to medical technicians, from gardeners to governors.

Miller helps individuals find the vocational fit that gives them the greatest satisfaction and joy, inspiring them to continue developing their lives along paths of fulfillment and significance. I will be tapping into this expertise to help you uncover your own areas of excellence.

In his book, *The Truth about You*, Miller says:

In order to discover a person's pattern, examine only those actions which he or she feels are accomplishments that resulted in personal satisfaction.... [These] accomplishments ... always have two basic elements: They are achievements which resulted in a feeling of satisfaction, regardless of what other people thought [and] they are achievements which the achiever felt were done well, regardless of their degree of significance in other people's eyes.

I like the fact that Miller does not view success as the world does. Many of the achievements that I believe are meaningful and important to God would be judged insignificant by the world's standards. As you examine your life, give yourself permission to claim achievements that brought you great levels of satisfaction, regardless of what others might think of them. God's delight and pride in you is not based on what is celebrated by the world.

Now, do some brainstorming, thinking of your past achievements/ experiences in these five areas:

1. *Personally*, you may have received an award that is especially meaningful to you.
2. *Vocationally*, perhaps you have a pattern of achievement when it comes to productivity, sales, or leadership.
3. *Relationally*, you may enjoy a godly marriage or benefit from a friendship that comforts you in difficult times or challenges you to strive for excellence in everything you do.
4. *Educationally*, perhaps you have academic degrees or training certificates, or perhaps you are pursuing ongoing development in areas of special interest.
5. *Spiritually*, you may have a history of success in sharing your faith or leading Christians to deeper insight about their own faith. Or perhaps your own acceptance of Christ and spiritual growth give you a sense of having attained something beyond measure.

Next, using brief phrases, identify at least three significant achievements in each area.

Personal Achievements:

1. _____

2. _____

3. _____

Vocational Achievements:

1. _____

2. _____

3. _____

Relational Achievements:

1. _____

2. _____

3. _____

Educational Achievements:

1. _____

2. _____

3. _____

Spiritual Achievements:

1. _____

2. _____

3. _____

Finally, review this list of fifteen positive experiences and select the top three. Once you have done this, use the empty picture frames on the next three pages to paint word portraits that showcase the significance of each event. Include all the facts of the event that you can remember and the feelings you experienced during this great time in your life. And give each portrait a title in the space provided at the bottom of the

frame. For example, were you to walk down the hallway of my life, you would see positive portraits entitled: *Father, I Want to Come Home*, which is what I said when I gave my life to Jesus; *My Angel*, a nickname for my wife, who brought me to faith during our dating season of life; and *Saddleback Church*, where I received God's call to serve him full-time as a pastor.

Putting Your Achievements to Work for God

Brad and Shelley have celebrated many years of marriage—a virtuous achievement for which they give glory to God. Grateful for God's gracious protection of their marriage, they use their experience to mentor young couples. The lessons these couples learn from Brad and Shelley enable them to remain Spirit-filled and steady when life's winds buffet.

After twenty years of leadership positions, Jeff now oversees a large portion of the United States for his company. This achievement has given him a platform to not only motivate his people so the company can grow, but also to model Christ to a lost world. One way Jeff models Christ is by not compromising his character when he encounters the temptations that frequently confront a traveling businessperson. Instead of dishonoring God with unworthy uses of his time, he uses it to pray for his team. He asks God to open doors so he can share his faith with them – a prayer God answers often.

When Tommy and Amy were falling in love, they made a commitment to honor God and each other by abstaining from physical intimacy until they were married. As difficult as it was, God gave them strength to keep that commitment – an achievement too seldom realized in our society today. Now that they are husband and wife, they use their experiences to help other young couples stay pure in the Lord's eyes prior to marriage.

My friend Katie, a bestselling author, is highly educated, with two masters degrees and a doctorate. Many people would become prideful about that much status and education, but Katie is one of the most humble individuals I know. She sees her accomplishments simply as door-openers for God to use. Her impressive resumé gives her frequent invitations to speak in a variety of settings around the world. She is only too happy to use those opportunities to share the good news of God's love with her listeners.

My wife, Stacey, is a great example of putting the positives from one's past to good use for God. Stacey grew up in an "Ozzie and Harriet" household. While my own childhood was dysfunctional, she knew what it was like to receive love, support, care, encouragement, and forgiveness from her Christ-centered parents. With that foundation, Stacey is able to pass on to our children what her mom and dad gave her. Her actions bless our children and even have filled in many missing pieces for me. Because of my precious wife, I have learned what it means to love, listen, and laugh as a couple and family.

The possibilities for your life achievements and experiences to become action steps for God are almost limitless. To help you begin to discover yours, review your three positive portraits and identify a few ways to build upon them to bless others and give God glory.

Next to each portrait, list one way that you could use this event from your past to help someone.

Painful Portraits

As much as we sometimes wish to ignore or deny it, the hallway of our lives has its difficult side as well. If you truly want to discover your uniqueness and be used by God in the process, you must be willing to take a hard look at these portraits of your painful experiences.

I'm not talking about the time that Barbie's or Batman's head broke off or your boyfriend or girlfriend broke up with you, but when your pain threshold was tested and your endurance was stretched to the breaking point. Divorce, abuse, death, alcoholism, cancer, depression, job loss, bankruptcy, eating disorders, miscarriages, suicide, abortion, affairs – the pain-producing possibilities are numerous.

As you journey down your hallway of life and focus on the painful side of your past, use the same five areas to identify specific points of pain.

Personal Points of Pain:

1. _____

2. _____

3. _____

Vocational Points of Pain:

1. _____

2. _____

3. _____

Relational Points of Pain:

1. _____

2. _____

3. _____

Educational Points of Pain:

1. _____

2. _____

3. _____

Spiritual Points of Pain:

1. _____

2. _____

3. _____

As before, review these fifteen difficult experiences and select the three most painful. Once you have done this, use the empty picture frames on pages 107–109 to paint word portraits (both facts and feelings) that bring detail to these significant events. And remember to name each portrait.

Letting Crisis Become a Catalyst

As I reflect on the painful portraits that hang down the hallway of my life, my memory is flooded with experiences that have shaped my life.

My parents divorced when I was eight, and my older brother and I had to live with our dad because my mom's salary as a grocery checker wasn't enough to support us. Dad drank excessively every night, then decided to share his inner pain with his sons. Most of the time Dad focused on me, the less-than-perfect student.

From verbal bombs that would shake anyone's self-worth to whippings that left welts and bruises, the pain came in many forms. Although the physical marks always healed, the verbal wounds on my soul were far deeper. The emotional intimidation and lack of affirmation finally ended when, at sixteen, I told Dad I was moving out. For many years, Dad had told me that if I would move out, he would pack my bags. That was one promise he kept—filling five large plastic garbage bags with my clothes and other personal items.

A friend once asked me, "Don't you wish you had never experienced that pain?" In one sense, even though my dad and I eventually reconciled and we now have a good relationship, I do wish I could erase that part of my life. But I also see it has made me the person I am today—emotionally stronger and better able to empathize with others in pain.

In *Shaped by God*, author Max Lucado uses a beautiful metaphor to describe the way God uses difficult experiences to form us:

> To melt down the old and recast it as new is a disrupting process. [But] with time, a change occurs: What was dull becomes sharpened, what was crooked becomes straight, what was weak becomes strong, and what was useless becomes valuable.
>
> Then the blacksmith ceases his pounding and sets down his hammer. In the still silence, he examines the smoking tool. The incandescent implement is rotated and examined for any mars or cracks.
>
> There are none.
>
> The pliable, soft mineral becomes an unbending, useful tool.

Lucado says, "God sees our life from beginning to end. He may lead us through a storm at age thirty so we can endure a hurricane at age sixty. An instrument is useful only if it's in the right shape. A dull ax or a bent screwdriver needs attention, and so do we. A good blacksmith keeps his tools in shape. So does God."

While I didn't have the healthiest role models or much-needed attention and affirmation as I was growing up, I'm grateful that God today gives me opportunities to work with men and women scarred by similar pain. Who better to help them than someone who has journeyed through it before—and survived? Because of my painful childhood, my heart is sensitive to them. God has graced me with the gift of encouragement, and I use it on a daily basis to help others. I don't think I would be as grateful and surrendered today if all my emotional needs had been met when I was a kid.

I'm reminded of Carrie, who helps teenage girls deal with unplanned pregnancies in a way that honors God. When she was young, Carrie didn't choose a God-honoring path. She has suffered with the consequences of that decision for many years. God's presence in her life today compels her to spare others the anguish of a wrong choice. Carrie knows God's power to transform a life, and because of that she is able to exert a healthy influence with these girls. She is an example of someone living the words of Jonathan Swift: "A man should never be ashamed to own he has been in the wrong. In other words, that he is wiser today than he was yesterday."

Then there is Paul, whose life was filled with tremendous pain and confusion when his wife left him for three months. He discovered that all he could do was to cling to God. Since his church had no support group to help him during his time of need, he started one so other men wouldn't feel alone in their pain. Now, because of the pain he endured, Paul has a significant ministry to men who are separated from their wives.

My friend Sandra lost her twenty-four-year-old daughter in a tragic automobile accident. Today she uses the pain of her daughter's death to mentor young women toward decisions that reflect the will of God. She recently took the lessons of her grief on a mission trip to Africa, where she helped pastors understand how to help people who suffer loss to find hope in Jesus. In her daughter's memory, she is even writing books for children, guiding them toward godly character choices.

What about you? Look back over the painful portraits of your life and think about the good that could come from your suffering. Then, next to each word portrait you've created, note how you might use that event to help someone else.

Will you choose to use your painful life experiences in a new way? Max Lucado makes another vital point when he writes, "Being tested by God reminds us that our function and task is to be about his business, that our purpose is to be an extension of his nature, an ambassador of his throne room, and a proclaimer of his message." Let your life proclaim his message, whether its content is marked by ease or adversity.

Before our experiences – positive or painful – can be fully used by God for the benefit of others, we must let go of their hold over our lives. Until we fully yield control of our lives to God, we'll remain stuck in neutral, road-blocked and getting nowhere fast. As we begin a new section of the book, in chapter 7 we'll examine the importance of giving everything to God.

GRABBING HOLD

Listen to your life. See it for the fathomless mystery it is,
in the boredom and pain of it no less than in the excitement and gladness:
touch, taste, smell your way to the holy and hidden heart of it because
in the last analysis all moments are key moments, and life itself is grace.

Frederick Buechner

Reflect on what you have learned. What are a few things you found out about God from this chapter?

Realize what you have been given. How have you discovered that there is purpose in your past?

Request help from others. Who are two people from whom you can seek help to overcome unhealthy patterns or trends in your life?

Respond in faith. Identify two action steps you can take in the next month to use your pain for God's gain.

1. _____

_____

2. _____

_____

Unlocking Your Life

Chapter 7

LETTING GO

Removing Roadblocks to a Surrendered Soul

The more we get what we now call "ourselves" out of the way
and let him take us over, the more truly ourselves we become.
C. S. Lewis

The absolute surrender of everything into his hands is necessary.
If our hearts are willing for that, there is no limit
to what God will do for us or to the blessing he will bestow.
Andrew Murray

God wants you to give him everything!

My wife, Stacey, and I love running. We count ourselves among those misguided souls who actually enjoy pounding their feet against hard surfaces for hours on end. Indeed, our friends would say we are more than a little dedicated!

One year Stacey, the faster between us, decided to run a full marathon — 26.2 miles. You won't see me lining up to run one, but I did enjoy training with Stacey. She trains in order to build up her endurance so she can finish the course strong, rather than beginning powerfully only to end the race barely breathing.

According to the writer of Hebrews, endurance is just as vital when it comes to our spiritual journey. And just how do we manage such stamina? Listen to his words: "Therefore, since we are surrounded by such a huge crowd of witnesses to the life of faith, let us strip off every weight that slows us down, especially the sin that so easily hinders our progress. And let us run with endurance the race that God has set before us. We do this by keeping our eyes on Jesus, on whom our faith depends from start to finish" (Hebrews 12:1–2, NLT).

Briefly put, we're to remove all of the excess *stuff* that distracts us and slows our pace. As runners in the race of life, our focus needs to be on Christ alone.

Our human tendency is to believe we possess the ability to unclog our lives without God having to plunge his hands into the thick of it all. The truth is, however, that the greatest obstacle to God fulfilling his purpose for our lives is not other people but ourselves — our own goals, ambition, pride, and self-will. Although it's difficult to comprehend, God, in his amazing grace, actually *yearns* for his children to hand off this deadweight. Yet we so often insist on carrying it with our own limited strength. In his book *Absolute Surrender*, Andrew Murray points out, "The first step in absolute surrender is to believe that God accepts your surrender."

It would be extremely foolish if my wife decided to show up at that marathon wearing boots and a weighted backpack. The inappropriate shoes would constantly be distracting her and the extra weight would slow her down, potentially causing her to bow out of the race early, not to mention cause serious injuries.

Like a literal race, the unhealthy choice on our part would be to run the race of life with all sorts of distractions and excess baggage slowing us down. That, of course, is Satan's plan. The longer you or I carry a burden, the longer it will hang on for the free ride, oblivious to the fact we are gasping for breath.

The apostle Paul tells us clearly that every believer in Jesus needs to surrender his or her life to God daily and resolve to be a living sacrifice for him (see Romans 12:1). It's only the surrendered heart that God can guide toward his Kingdom Purpose.

Observes a pastor friend, Brad Johnson: "Give God a man buried in the snow of Valley Forge and God will make a Washington. Give God a man born in abject poverty and God will stand him in front of a nation and make a Lincoln. Give God a man born black in a society filled with discrimination and God will make a Martin Luther King Jr. Give God a child called unable to learn and God will make an Einstein."

When you think of the word *surrender*, what comes to your mind? Maybe you picture someone yielding to authorities following a car chase, an opponent admitting defeat after a fight, or the sense of relief that results from giving up a destructive habit. What I'm talking about here, however, is not a physical position or an emotional feeling, but the spiritual position of our soul that enables us to authentically display the characteristics of Christ—traits such as love, peace, patience, joy, and self-control.

We surrender when we hand off *every* aspect of our lives—past, present, and future—to God and trust him completely with all of it. Think of it as passing the baton of your life to the ultimate Life Source and asking him, in return, to give you the power to live for him every day.

The Bible gives us a challenging picture of this idea through Jesus' words: "If any of you wants to be my follower,... you must put aside your selfish ambition, shoulder your cross, and follow me" (Mark 8:34, NLT). Jesus' instruction is laid out in such a simplified form that I think we're all curious why he thought these tasks would be so doable. But the fact is, if Jesus did not know with certainty that we would be able to follow him in this manner with the force of the Holy Spirit helping us, he would not have called us to such an extreme and elevated way of living.

A word of caution as you read further into this chapter: the process of surrendering—what the Bible calls transformation—is far from instantaneous and is often accompanied by pain. Armed with this truth, I urge you not to shy away from the honor of being transformed for God's use. Satan wants you and me to be intimidated by the process of surrendering. He knows that sense of intimidation will keep us from willingly offering our lives and our S.H.A.P.E. to God, and his number-one goal—once he knows he has lost us eternally—is to render us ineffective for God.

David G. Benner writes in his book, *Surrender to Love*:

> The key to spiritual transformation is meeting God ... in vulnerability. Our natural inclination is to bring the most presentable parts of our self to the encounter with God. But God wants us to bring our whole self to the divine encounter. He wants us to trust him enough to meet Perfect Love in the vulnerability of our shame, weakness and sin....
> Tragically, however, most of us have large tracts of our inner world that are excluded from God's transforming love and friendship. Perpetuating such exclusions limits our conversion. It is like going to the doctor for a checkup and denying any problems, focusing on the parts of oneself that are most healthy.

If we wish to move forward in the surrender process, such a reaction would be counterproductive. Coming to God—just as we are—is absolutely instrumental in gaining a fresh and unburdened beginning.

Your Surrender Moment

Have you surrendered everything to God? By everything, I mean *everything*: relationships, careers, kids, money, dreams, desires, pain, regret, worry, longings—everything that makes up your life or that you long to see included in your life plan. Ask God if there are things in your life that you are not allowing him to have complete control over.

This section is meant to bring to the surface the things in your life that are distracting you and slowing you down from living out your Kingdom Purpose. As Max Lucado has said, "Don't go to God with options and expect him to choose one of your preferences. Go to him with empty hands—

no hidden agendas, no crossed fingers, nothing behind your back. Go to him with a willingness to do whatever he says. If you surrender your will, then he will 'equip you with everything good for doing his will.'"

While surrendering—the process of giving ourselves over to God's way—is a lifelong challenge, most believers can point to a particular point in time—a "surrender moment"—when they first acknowledged that God alone has the right to sit on the throne. My own surrender moment was unplanned—at least on my part. Although years prior I had asked Jesus to be the boss of my life, there were still areas where I had not given up ownership. During a devotional time at a life-planning event in 1998, the instructor read from Psalm 139 and then began explaining the act of releasing everything in our lives to God. Doing that, he said, enabled God to take his rightful place as the center of our lives. As he read the Psalm, my heart started racing. Thoughts both good and bad flooded my mind.

Tears filled my eyes as he read: "Search me, O God, and know my heart; test me and know my anxious thoughts. See if there is any offensive way in me, and lead me in the way everlasting" (Psalm 139:23–24). I actually felt God searching my heart. He began pointing out all the areas he wanted me to release to him. As God took inventory of my soul, the instructor challenged us to surrender entirely by giving up all areas of our lives to Christ.

The next thing I knew, I was standing up and shouting, "I surrender!" in front of people whose names I didn't even know. The instructor came over, laid his hands on my shoulder, and asked others to surround me for prayer. I wish I could say I remember exactly what was prayed over me, but what I do vividly remember is the feeling of hands pressing against my back as they prayed. The body of Christ, a group of believers, ministered to a member in need as my worries, wrongs, and past wounds poured out. I can always look back to that day and know I left totally surrendered to God. I will never forget it.

The concept of surrender is woven thoroughly through the Bible. Rick Warren writes in *The Purpose Driven® Life*:

[The apostle] Paul's moment of surrender occurred on the Damascus road after he was knocked down by blinding light. For others, God gets our attention with less drastic methods. Regardless, surrendering is never just a one-time event. Paul said, "I die *daily*" (1 Corinthians

15:51). There is a *moment* of surrender, and there is the *practice* of surrender, which is moment-by-moment and lifelong. The problem with a *living* sacrifice is that it can crawl off the altar, so you may have to resurrender your life fifty times a day. You must make it a daily habit. Jesus said, "If people want to follow me, they must give up the things they want. They must be willing to give up their lives daily to follow me" (Luke 9:23, New Century Version).

Have *you* ever given *all* of your life to God? Or have you given pieces to God and then ended up taking them back? No matter where you are, establish your surrender moment right now. Ask God to reveal the things in your life that are weighing you down and distracting you from being the masterpiece he made you to be.

To help you accomplish this goal, let's examine five roadblocks of life that are crucial for letting go of your past—worries, wounds, wrongs, weaknesses, and wishes. But before we begin, I'd like to pray for you:

> *Dear God, please help this wonderful creation of yours to survey their life right now. Show them everything that slows them down and distracts them from you. Give them the strength to give those things to you. Take every aspect of their life and use it for your glory. Help them feel your love, acceptance, grace, and forgiveness in a new and fresh way. Give them a clean start with you today. In Jesus' name, Amen.*

Give God Your Worries

If we tried to identify one worldwide, unifying human characteristic, I suspect it would be living in anxiety or, as we call it today, "stress." Many people are stressed out over many things these days.

Everyone is affected by worry or stress to some degree. For some, it's an occasional thing prompted by extraordinary circumstances. Many others, however, are *chronic* worriers. They spend their days mulling over all the things they want to control or fix, but cannot. After a while, this constant carrying of our own burdens weighs us down and distances us from God.

The Bible tells us God wants our worries: "Cast your cares on the LORD and he will sustain you; he will never let the righteous fall" (Psalm 55:22). The word *cast* does not mean to merely hand our cares to God.

Instead, God is telling us to *heave* them at him. It's as if he is saying, "Bring it on! I can take it. Give them to me. I want them all. They're not going to weigh me down."

The question then becomes, "What are you worried about?" The people I commonly counsel are worried about work, relationships, finances, health issues, or not seeing their desires come to pass. Others worry about being accepted, overcoming sinful patterns, feeling that they are forgiven by God, or being given a purpose they feel they cannot carry out.

Billy Graham reminds us, "Anxiety is the natural result when our hopes are centered in anything short of God and his will for us." Our hopes and plans for our lives are the very things that, when taken out of perspective, lead to anxious thoughts and emotions.

If you were to peek into my "worry ledger," you would see one major entry: my family. My wife and I have been blessed with two beautiful girls and a handsome young boy, and as their dad, I care about them deeply. My experience growing up in a dysfunctional family causes me to worry about my ability to raise a Christ-centered family. When it comes to being the husband God calls me to be, I worry. When it comes to being the dad my children deserve, I worry. Because my dad has been married and divorced three times, the statistics are against me. "Experts" would say my marriage isn't likely to work. The fear they may be right drives me to God constantly, begging him for wisdom and strength. Because I long to have a marriage that brings glory to him, I regularly ask him to keep me from succumbing to worry.

What about you? Use the space below to list the worries of your life. Once finished, give the items on it to God.

Give God Your Wounds

Along with your worries, God also wants your wounds. He's waiting for you to trust him with those things in your life that have brought you the greatest pain and caused lasting scars. Even if you believe the damage done is irreparable, Scripture says, "He heals the brokenhearted and binds up their wounds" (Psalm 147:3).

Someone once told me, "God doesn't want to rub it in, he wants to rub it out." Our loving heavenly Father wants to take our wounds and help us overcome them. Physical wounds, of course, usually heal. What I'm referring to is something deeper, something inside your heart. I've found that in my life – as well as the lives of many I've come in contact with – emotional injuries don't heal quickly. Often that's because we have not taken God at his word. He has told us he is the Great Physician. He promises he will heal our wounds.

"Jane" suffered as horrible a wound as anyone can imagine. After drinking too much at a New Year's party, she passed out. When she came to, she was being raped.

"I thought I was having a nightmare," she says. "I fought as hard as I could, but there was nothing I could do. When the stranger was done, he simply got up and left. I felt so helpless and violated. I was at a loss as to how to cope. So I stuck the experience in a corner and decided to never think about it again.

"A little over a year later, I married a wonderful man. Suddenly I found myself in a relationship that was supposed to be sexually intimate and loving. It brought back a flood of feelings about that night – feelings I had never allowed myself to come to terms with. It had never occurred to me that I would feel as though my husband was raping me every night.

"I forced myself to begin talking about things, and little by little the pain began to lessen. The hardest part wasn't forgiving the guy who raped me; it was forgiving *myself.* I couldn't shake the little voice that kept telling me, 'You were drunk again. You chose to be there.' Finally I cried out to God: 'Lord, I'm so sick of hearing these damaging words in my head. Would you forgive me for drinking too much that night? Would you forgive me for not making the right choices?'

"I felt instantaneously free! I realized that Christ's pain on the cross was far bigger than what I had suffered. I realized that it wasn't all about me and my pain. From then on, my story wasn't even mine anymore. My story wasn't about a tragedy. It was about a victory. It wasn't even my victory—it was his. It hasn't been my life since then. It's been his. I honestly don't think there's anything greater."

Has someone hurt you so deeply that you can't stop thinking about the pain? Is there someone you say you never want to be like? Your bitterness makes you more like them than you know. The only way to find freedom and healing is to give the ache to God.

What emotional wounds are you carrying? It's time to allow God to heal them. Use the space below to indicate your wounds so you can surrender them completely to God.

Did you write anything? If not, go back and do so. Satan will whisper in your ear, "Don't let anybody know." That is a lie. God *already knows*. He wants you to speak his name and give him your hurts. Don't let those old wounds rob you of the future God has for you. Don't let them slow down or prevent the work you've been uniquely equipped to accomplish.

If you have serious wounds from your past that you feel have control over your life, please get help from a professional Christian counselor. You must learn to forgive the people from your past if you are going to truly maximize your life for God.

Give God Your Wrongs

Our wounds result from the actions of others, but our *wrongs* are things we have done to cause our own shame and distress, mistakes we've committed against someone else—either intentionally or unintentionally. Wrongs can come through our actions, our words, or both.

Naturally, we don't want to admit our wrongs. But God wants us to come clean so Christ can give us the rest that he provides: "Come to me, all you who are weary and burdened, and I will give you rest" (Matthew 11:28).

Very few things are more harmful than guilt when it comes to our attempts to fulfill our Kingdom Purpose. God is not the author of guilt in a Christian's life; that's Satan's trap. The Bible says there is no condemnation in Christ (see Romans 8:1). If you feel guilty about your attitude or actions toward others—sins for which Christ has already paid the price—refuse to give in to that destructive influence.

There is a difference, however, between guilt and conviction. Because God cares about us and our integrity, he will convict us of our sins. He wants us to repent and make our connection with him clean again. While guilt makes us feel unworthy and causes us to want to hide from God, conviction makes us feel worthy and urges us to run to God.

I'm not proud of it, but I have wounded people with my words. Even though I know the Bible says, "Everyone should be quick to listen, slow to speak and slow to become angry, for man's anger does not bring about the righteous life that God desires" (James 1:19–20), when I fail to let the Spirit lead my life, the result sometimes can be words that are displeasing to God and hurtful to others. Whether with words or actions, we've all offended.

Giving your wrongs to God starts with confession—the act of admitting our wrongs to God and to those we've hurt in order to receive forgiveness. True confession requires a sincerely repentant heart. It is not enough to make excuses for ourselves—trying to pass off our sin as a simple mistake. Doing that cheapens Christ's sacrifice. Corrie ten Boom once wrote, "The blood of Jesus never cleansed an excuse." I have had to confess to my wife attitudes and actions that were out of line and upsetting. I also have had to confess to my kids—the hardest thing for a parent to do—when I have not treated them with the respect they deserve from their dad.

The Bible tells us that if we confess, we receive forgiveness and purity from God: "If we confess our sins, he is faithful and just and will forgive us our sins and purify us from all unrighteousness" (1 John 1:9). But if it's true that God is aware (to say the least) of our wrongs before we come to him in confession, why do we need to do it? Frederick Buechner offers this explanation: "To confess your sins to God is not to tell him anything he doesn't already know. Until you confess them, however, they are the abyss between you. When you confess them, they become the bridge."

The Bible also warns us of the penalty for *not* confessing: "People who cover over their sins will not prosper. But if they confess and forsake them, they will receive mercy. Blessed are those who have a tender conscience, but the stubborn are headed for serious trouble" (Proverbs 28:13–14, NLT). Once again, God leaves us with a choice: confess our wrongs or hang on to them without being able to feel the sense of relief that comes with repentance.

In his book, *The Life You've Always Wanted,* John Ortberg says, "Confession is not primarily something God has us do because he needs it. God is not clutching tightly to his mercy, as if we have to pry it from his fingers like a child's last cookie. We need to confess in order to heal and be changed." That is the purpose of confession that God wants us to grasp.

What wounds have you caused in another person's life that you have not confessed to God and for which you have not asked for forgiveness from the person? List them below, confess them to God, and seek forgiveness if at all possible.

Give God Your Weaknesses

Do you ever brag about your weaknesses? In today's "you can do it all" society, it is totally countercultural even to talk about our weaknesses. Most of us love to talk about our strengths and downplay our weaknesses. I admit I do. But God wants us to embrace our weaknesses so we can be made strong in him.

The apostle Paul wrote,

> But to keep me from getting puffed up, I was given a thorn in my flesh, a messenger from Satan to torment me and keep me from getting proud. Three different times I begged the Lord to take it away. Each time he said, "My gracious favor is all you need. My power works best in your weakness." So now I am glad to boast about my weaknesses, so that the power of Christ may work through me (2 Corinthians 12:7–9, NLT).

When we operate out of our strengths, we often forget to include God, relying on our own abilities to accomplish tasks. But when we are asked to carry out tasks that require using what we consider our weak spots, our tendency is to go to God more quickly—and that's *exactly* what he wants.

Ron Mehl, a pastor and faithful friend of God until the Lord took him home following a two-decade battle with leukemia, once asked, "If we had no shortcomings, could there be overcomings?" Our Father wants us to be overcomers—with him leading us.

From the past to the present, God is still in the business of wanting to use our weaknesses for his glory. Take Rick Warren, for example. Those who know him from a distance would call him a great communicator, a visionary, a strategic thinker, an author, and a leader. In 2005 *Time* magazine actually highlighted him as one of the most influential people in America. All those things are true, but what is not as obvious about Rick is the way God uses his weaknesses in extraordinary ways.

Each time Rick speaks to crowds, the adrenaline rushes through his body—a common experience for most public speakers. But Rick is allergic to adrenaline. It actually causes him to be unable to see for a short period of time. You might think somebody who was affected like that would say, "God, you've made a mistake. No more speaking for me." But Rick continually chooses to not give this weakness a foothold because he knows that giving in to it would keep him from fulfilling his Kingdom Purpose. Rick talks regularly about this weakness. He knows that without God's strength he could not do what he does. God is glorified through Rick's weakness.

Pastor Brad Johnson observes, "Broken soil brings wheat, broken clouds bring rain, broken bread brings strength, and a broken person is what God chooses to use for his purposes."

God wants to use you too. You may think you have a weakness too great to be used, but God promises that he will use it in a way that blesses others and glorifies him if you put it in his hands. It flies in the face of human logic, but God wants to use *all* of us. The only thing that stops him from doing that is our unwillingness to give it all to him.

What are you holding on to, certain God has no use for it? Hand each weakness over to God (list them here) and let God amaze you.

Give God Your Wishes

God also longs for you to give him your dreams, desires, and wishes. He wants to bless your socks off and use you in a mighty way—but he can't do that unless you trust him with these things as well. The Bible says, "Trust in the LORD with all your heart; do not depend on your own understanding. Seek his will in all you do, and he will direct your paths" (Proverbs 3:5–6, NLT). The more we trust God with our lives, the clearer our path becomes. Eventually we are able to find and fulfill our Kingdom Purpose.

My wife would tell you that I don't run short of wishes. My mind is a swarm of dreams and desires, some for myself and others for God. I thank the Lord for my wife, who lets me know when my wishes are too focused on myself.

One of my personal safeguards against that tendency is to ask myself, "Who is the primary beneficiary of this wish?" If I recognize it only works to my advantage, I try to cut short my pursuit of that particular desire. If it's clear my wish is meant to benefit God and others, I seek wisdom from my friends and pray over the idea until I have peace about what to do next. While this system is far from perfect, I have learned that seeking God first saves a lot of wasted time and energy. The Bible says, "But seek first his kingdom and his righteousness, and all these things will be given to you as well" (Matthew 6:33).

Dreams can be great things. Bruce Wilkinson writes in his book *The Dream Giver*, "God has put a driving passion in you to do something special. Why wouldn't He? You are created in His image—the only person exactly like you in the universe. No one else can do your Dream." However, he goes on to remind us, "If you don't surrender your Dream, you will be placing it higher on your priority list than God. Your Dream is meant to be about more than itself or you. A God-given Dream brings you together with what God wants to do in His world *through you*."

So, what are those wishes, dreams, and desires that *you* need to surrender today? List them now.

Let It Go

This chapter is by far the most difficult in this book because it forces us to look deep into our souls. That can hurt—*a lot*. But when we admit our "stuff" to God and ask for forgiveness from him and from others, we discover we've been released from bondage. For the first time in our lives, we can enjoy freedom of mind, body, and soul. We can stop competing and comparing and start contributing solely for him. And God is finally free to begin completing his masterpiece in our lives.

Rick Warren writes:

> You know you're surrendered to God when you rely on God to work things out instead of trying to manipulate others, force your agenda, and control the situation. You let go and let God work. You don't have to always be "in charge." The Bible says, "Surrender yourself to the Lord, and wait patiently for him" (Psalm 37:7a, GWT). Instead of trying harder, you trust more. You also know you're surrendered when you don't react to criticism and rush to defend yourself. Surrendered hearts show up best in relationships. You don't edge others out, you don't demand your rights, and you aren't self-serving when you're surrendered.

If you have never had your surrender moment, make this it. Don't be afraid of taking this important step, and don't listen to Satan's lie that it's not really necessary. The Bible is very clear that the only thing we are to fear is God: "Do not fear anything except the LORD Almighty. He alone is the Holy One. If you fear him, you need fear nothing else. He will keep you safe" (Isaiah 8:13–14, NLT). Step out in faith. Then, do whatever it takes to make sure your surrender to God remains secure. One way to do this is by sharing your commitment with a close friend or family member and making yourselves accountable to each other.

Have you ever met someone you just *knew* had a surrendered soul? You can see it in a person's life, in their placing the needs of others above their own. People who live to please God by putting others' needs first are called "servants." In the next chapter, we'll put a spiritual stethoscope on this servant heart and listen to its distinctive rhythm.

GRABBING HOLD

Reflect on what you have learned. What are a few things you have learned about surrender from this chapter?

Realize what you have been given. You have been given the opportunity to secure your surrender sign. Don't wait another moment. Do it now. Use the space below to write God your personal surrender prayer that includes all the items (worries, wounds, wrongs, weaknesses, wishes) in your life that you need to give completely to him.

> *Dear God, today I'm fully surrendering my life to you. I realize that I have been holding things back from you, for which I'm sorry. Please take from me all of the things I have listed below and give me the rest that your Word promises. In addition, give me the strength and wisdom to live surrendered every day of my life.*
>
> *God I surrender the following to you today . . .*

Request help from others. Who are two people in your life who can help keep your soul surrendered for God?

Respond in faith. Contact the two people you listed above and let them know about your surrender moment.

Chapter 8

OTHER-CENTERED

Responding with a Generous Heart

Whatever you do, work at it with all your heart,
as working for the Lord, not for men,
since you know that you will receive an inheritance
from the Lord as a reward.
It is the Lord Christ you are serving.
Colossians 3:23–24

I see life as both a gift and a responsibility.
My responsibility is to use what God has given me
to help his people in need.
Millard Fuller, founder of Habitat for Humanity

Live beyond yourself.

At about 2 a.m. on Saturday, March 12, 2005, Ashley Smith decided to drive to a local market to buy some cigarettes. On the way, she thought happily about picking up her five-year-old daughter from a church event later that morning. She had no idea her quiet life was about to change forever.

Back home, Ashley got out of her car—and was immediately accosted by a man with a gun. Hours earlier, rape suspect Brian Nichols allegedly had shot his way out of an Atlanta courthouse, leaving a judge and three others dead in his wake. He held Ashley at gunpoint, forced his way into her home, and tied her up.

The next seven hours felt like seven years. Because of the televised jailbreak, Ashley knew Brian was wanted for cold-blooded killings. She struggled to control her fear, sure she was going to die.

When her husband, Mack, was murdered in 2001, Ashley was a Christian but living far from Jesus. After Mack's death, the drug crystal methamphetamine formed a strong hold on her. Eventually, her life was in such disarray that she gave custody of her daughter, Paige, to her aunt. When Brian Nichols took her hostage, she had started rebuilding her life—working and going to school, getting her own apartment, and looking forward to regaining custody of Paige. Every day she read a chapter from *The Purpose Driven® Life*. Yet, though she didn't use drugs constantly anymore, she still struggled with addiction. When Brian asked Ashley if she had marijuana, she said she didn't—but she offered him the crystal methamphetamine she did have. Nichols asked her to use the drug with him.

"I really didn't think God was going to give me another chance," Ashley said later. "So what I did was surrender completely to him and say, 'You probably are going to take me home tonight, and before you take me home, I need to get right with you.' In doing that, God did give me another chance."

Ashley recognized Brian as a man desperately in need of Christ. He needed to know what Jesus looked like and to experience his limitless grace. She allowed the Holy Spirit to take control. She served Brian pancakes and they talked, just like normal people do. They talked, among other things, about the Bible and *The Purpose Driven® Life*. Brian asked Ashley to read it to him, so she picked up where she'd left off in her own daily reading. It turned out to be Day 33: "How Real Servants Act." Its focus is on living your life others-centered, allowing God to interrupt your life for the sake of someone else.

Ashley told Brian how she'd been widowed and explained that if he hurt her, her daughter would be without either a daddy or mommy. Quietly, gently, the Holy Spirit acted. Brian hung curtains for Ashley, then let her leave to pick up her daughter. She called 9-1-1 and Brian Nichols surrendered peacefully to police.

Dietrich Bonhoeffer once observed, "It is part of the discipline of humility that we must not spare our hand where it can perform a service and that we do not assume that our schedule is our own to manage, but allow it to be arranged by God." Ashley got an object lesson that night in exactly what Bonhoeffer meant. Whether we've yielded our lives to God or not, this much is true: our schedules really are not our own. When we put them in God's hands, we may discover—as Ashley Smith did that night—that interruptions, no matter how unwelcome, can be turned into opportunities to minister.

The star of this story is not Ashley Smith. The central character is a heart—specifically, a servant's heart. Because Ashley chose to think "others-centered," rather than "self-centered," her courage shined powerfully under a pressure most of us will never know—in spite of her own human weakness. Faith gave her the strength to serve someone others might have shunned or cowered from in fear for their lives.

Ashley modeled the words of Jesus to his disciples: "But among you it should be quite different. Whoever wants to be a leader among you must be your servant, and whoever wants to be first must become your slave. For even I, the Son of Man, came here not to be served but to serve others, and to give my life as a ransom for many" (Matthew 20:26–28, NLT). Christ made it clear that servanthood is not only an honorable characteristic, it is mandatory for one who claims to be his disciple.

Devotional writer Gerald Hartis says, "Ministry is what we leave in our wake as we follow Jesus." By choosing the servant nature of Christ,

Ashley Smith left in her wake a powerful testament to his power. You too will leave a wake as you strive to serve others through your S.H.A.P.E.

Someone once said, "Your theology is what you are when the talking stops and the action starts." What we believe is demonstrated by what we do, not just by what we say. Good intentions are not enough—they must be followed by deeds that demonstrate they are true.

As Jesus traveled, he served—helping, healing, and laying a hand whenever there was a need. He humbled himself in front of his own followers when he washed their feet—one of the lowest positions a person in that time could assume. He even took the role of servant all the way to death—obeying God's will in spite of what it would cost him personally.

God is not looking for perfectly manicured hands. His delight is in weathered and callused hands that demonstrate a "whatever it takes" attitude. That was precisely the challenge Paul issued to the church at Philippi: "Each of you should look not only to your own interests, but also to the interests of others. Your attitude should be the same as that of Christ Jesus: Who, being in very nature God, did not consider equality with God something to be grasped, but made himself nothing, taking the very nature of a servant, being made in human likeness" (Philippians 2:4–7).

Ashley's story can motivate us to maximize our lives by living beyond ourselves. It's not likely any of us will find ourselves in a situation like hers, but as believers in Christ we can count on a lifetime of opportunities to serve others and share our faith. Jesus wants us to make our faith known through serving others, like Ashley did for Brian—and like a man we know only as "the Good Samaritan" did thousands of years ago.

The Story of the Good Samaritan

(Luke 10:25–37)

On one occasion an expert in the law stood up to test Jesus. "Teacher," he asked, "what must I do to inherit eternal life?"

"What is written in the Law?" [Jesus] replied. "How do you read it?"

[The man] answered: "'Love the Lord your God with all your heart and with all your soul and with all your strength and with all your mind'; and, 'Love your neighbor as yourself.'"

"You have answered correctly," Jesus replied. "Do this and you will live."

But he wanted to justify himself, so he asked Jesus, "And who is my neighbor?"

In reply Jesus said: "A man was going down from Jerusalem to Jericho, when he fell into the hands of robbers. They stripped him of his clothes, beat him and went away, leaving him half dead. A priest happened to be going down the same road, and when he saw the man, he passed by on the other side. So too, a Levite, when he came to the place and saw him, passed by on the other side. But a Samaritan, as he traveled, came where the man was; and when he saw him, he took pity on him. He went to him and bandaged his wounds, pouring on oil and wine. Then he put the man on his own donkey, took him to an inn and took care of him. The next day he took out two silver coins and gave them to the innkeeper. 'Look after him,' he said, 'and when I return, I will reimburse you for any extra expense you may have.'

"Which of these three do you think was a neighbor to the man who fell into the hands of robbers?"

The expert in the law replied, "The one who had mercy on him."

Jesus told him, "Go and do likewise."

■ ■ ■ ■ ■

Now let's take a close-up look at various aspects of this well known parable of Jesus to learn fresh lessons about using what God has given us to serve others.

Use Your Mind to Think Like a Servant

Servanthood starts by thinking like a servant. Scripture tells us that a servant thinks only about the approval of his or her master. "Whatever you do, work at it with all your heart, as working for the Lord, not for men, since you know that you will receive an inheritance from the Lord as a reward. It is the Lord Christ you are serving" (Colossians 3:23–24). I know that is totally countercultural, but you and I must live for an audience of one.

The Good Samaritan thought about the needs of others before dwelling on his own needs. I once heard it said, "The body never goes where the mind has never been." If your mind is set on serving others, then you will act on that purpose. There is no way the Good Samaritan would have responded to this person in need if he had not thought beforehand about the importance of serving others. His first step toward the man in need was taken in his mind.

Thinking like a servant also provides the strength the servant needs to be content with his life, without having to compare himself with others — and being overcome with the pride or pity that inevitably results. By tempting you to get out your spiritual yardstick, Satan will trick you into getting your mind off Jesus and onto your own concerns.

Martin Luther King Jr. encouraged us to see whatever God hands us as our contribution and calling. No matter what role he puts us in, our responsibility to the Father is to bring him pride as we do it. King said, "If a man is called to be a street-sweeper, he should sweep streets even as Michelangelo painted, or Beethoven composed music, or Shakespeare wrote poetry. He should sweep streets so well that all the hosts of heaven and earth will pause to say, 'Here lived a great street-sweeper who did his job well.'"

Comparison, whether out of pride or embarrassment, will not help us keep our minds servant-focused. Acceptance will.

Use Your Ears to Hear Like a Servant

God not only wants you to *think* like a servant, he also wants you to *listen* for opportunities to serve. Servants are attentive because that is a characteristic of God: "The eyes of the LORD are on the righteous and his ears are attentive to their cry" (Psalm 34:15). God is listening to our cries and expects us to listen to the cries of others as well. The Samaritan was so sensitive toward the needs of others that a cry for help would have touched his heart. We also need to have our ears tuned for cries for help, whether they are loud and insistent or subtle and nuanced.

One day Joe came to meet with me. When I asked him how things were going, he said, "Great!" But every time I asked about his wife, his tone of voice changed. I decided to get more specific: "How's your marriage, Joe — *really*?" Joe finally told me his wife had committed adultery. Needless to say, he wasn't doing well at all. Joe needed help, and God gave me ears to hear his cry.

Perhaps you have had a similar experience with a family member, friend, or coworker. If you are listening, God will give you many opportunities to serve.

Use Your Eyes to See Like a Servant

When the Samaritan saw the man in need, he cared and responded with an act of love. Remember Jesus' own servant vision: "When he saw the crowds, he had compassion on them, because they were harassed and helpless, like sheep without a shepherd" (Matthew 9:36). Just like the Samaritan, just like Jesus, God gave you eyes to see. He wants you to use them in service to others, in ways that glorify him.

Perhaps there have been times you *thought* about meeting someone else's need, but when you actually faced a real situation, you retreated out of fear or pride. I've found a simple motto that captures the heart of a true servant: "Spot it, you got it." That is the attitude that made the Good Samaritan someone we remember to this day. He spotted the need and took action. Rather than wait around for someone else to act, he made the first move.

Keep your eyes open for opportunities to serve others with love.

Use Your Words to Speak Like a Servant

The Scripture instructs us to show kindness to others: "Therefore, as God's chosen people, holy and dearly loved, clothe yourselves with compassion, kindness, humility, gentleness and patience. Bear with each other and forgive whatever grievances you may have against one another. Forgive as the Lord forgave you. And over all these virtues put on love, which binds them all together in perfect unity" (Colossians 3:12 – 14). The Samaritan bore the burdens of the wounded man. You can help people in need with nothing more than your words.

God wants us to use our words to serve others. He wants us to go beyond simple actions and speak healing and hope into the lives around us, verbally lifting them out of their pain and brokenness. His Word teaches in Proverbs 16:24: "Pleasant words are a honeycomb, sweet to the soul and healing to the bones." Think of times in your own life when someone said something kind and uplifting that put wind in your sails (versus times when another's words drained the joy from you). Challenge yourself to be a dispenser of verbal medicine—an encourager who speaks healing into another person's life.

Use Your Heart to Love Like a Servant

The Samaritan's heart overflowed with love for God—a power rippling inside him that allowed him to love others. Bob Pierce, founder of World Vision and Samaritan's Purse, said, "Let my heart be broken by the things that break the heart of God." The Good Samaritan lived by that principle.

The Bible says, "And all of you, serve each other in humility, for 'God sets himself against the proud, but he shows favor to the humble'" (1 Peter 5:5, NLT). If we want God's favor on our lives, we must be humble. Charles Spurgeon said, "Humility is the proper estimate of oneself." To get an honest view of ourselves, we must look to only one source—Christ himself—who says, "Whoever wants to be great must become a servant" (Matthew 20:26b, MSG). As Rick Warren notes, greatness in God's book is not measured by how many people serve you, but by how many people you serve.

In his classic book, *Humility*, Andrew Murray writes:

He [Jesus] simply taught us the blessed truth that there is nothing so divine and heavenly as being the servant and helper of all. The faithful servant, who recognizes his position, finds real pleasure in supplying the wants of the master or his guests. When we see that humility is something infinitely deeper than sorrow, and accept it as our participation in the life of Jesus, we shall begin to learn that it is our true nobility, and that to prove it in being servants of all is the highest fulfillment of our destiny, as men created in the image of God.

John Ortberg points out our natural tendency to want all eyes on us, even when it comes to serving and showing humility while we serve: "We'd like to be humble ... but what if no one notices?" And there's the paradox. We all have chances to serve every day, but, as Thomas Edison once pointed out, "Opportunity is missed by most people because it is dressed in overalls and looks like work."

Use Your Resources to Give Like a Servant

The Good Samaritan didn't stop with just offering words of comfort and bandaging the injured man's wounds. God's Word tells us that he took the man to an inn, stayed with him overnight, then paid the innkeeper the equivalent of two day's wages—with a promise to pay even more for the stranger's expenses beyond that amount.

Like the Good Samaritan, a servant uses whatever resources are available to show God's love in practical ways. Servants see money as a tool to bless others. Abraham Lincoln once wrote, "To ease another's heartache is to forget one's own."

God is a giver. It's his nature. He gave his one and only son, Jesus, so that, through faith in him, we can experience forgiveness of our sin and have eternal life with God. This one, sacred act should be all the proof we need.

He gave you your life as well. The Bible says we are made in God's image, so if God is a giver, that means we're created *by* him to give *like* him. Scripture contains more than two thousand references to giving—more than all the references to faith, hope, and love—making it clear the Bible puts more emphasis on giving and generosity than any other principle.

Life is all about giving, not getting. The truth is, we won't find our lives until we give them away. "Give away your life; you'll find life given back, but not merely given back—given back with bonus and blessing. Giving, not getting, is the way. Generosity begets generosity" (Luke 6:38, MSG). God wants to bless us as we give up our lives for him and serve others. Part of this giving is using your S.H.A.P.E. to serve and bless others, which is how God wants you to fulfill your Kingdom Purpose.

Significance Starts with Service

Each year at our staff Christmas party, we hand out what we like to call the "Significant Servant Award." This special recognition is for the one person who goes way beyond his or her job to serve others, while always keeping a low profile and never taking credit for his work. Year after year, one staff member is consistently recognized. Bob is an incredible model of servanthood. If you ask him to do something, his reply is always, "You bet. We will get right on it."

Bob's love for God and his desire to serve reminds me of Paul's instructions to the church at Ephesus: "Work hard, but not just to please your masters when they are watching. As slaves of Christ, do the will of God with all your heart. Work with enthusiasm, as though you were working for the Lord rather than for people. Remember that the Lord will reward each one of us for the good we do" (Ephesians 6:6–8, NLT). One day, Bob will be richly rewarded for his labor of love for God.

Bob always and immediately thinks about serving others before himself. His ears are always open to their requests, while his eyes constantly look for serving opportunities around the church. Bob's heart is full of God's love and grace, and it shows every time he serves. Bob is dedicated, attentive, loving, compassionate, humble, and generous—all at the same time. He demonstrates the spirit of a Samaritan: head, heart, hands, and feet—all in motion, serving God.

God designed us to serve one another—and you can't live out that purpose unless you are with others! No matter what you've thought up to now, you're not meant to be a "Lone Ranger" Christian. In the next chapter, we'll talk about how to build a support system—a caring community—around you. With the right team on your side, you'll be amazed at what God can do through you.

Reflect on what you have learned. What are a few things you have learned about God from this chapter?

Realize what you have been given. How can you use your hands to serve someone this week?

Request help from others. Think of three people in your life who model servanthood. Ask them how they keep their hearts in that position. Note any new insights you receive.

Respond in faith. What are two steps of faith you can take to model the life of the Good Samaritan?

1. _____

_____

2. _____

_____

Chapter 9

BETTER TOGETHER

Requesting Help from Others

So encourage each other and build each other up.

1 Thessalonians 5:11a (NLT)

We are better together.

Rick Warren

You need a team.

Longing to explore other possibilities for his life, Jeff decided to sell his share of the business to his partner. For six months, however, Jeff found nothing but closed doors. What had gone wrong? Had he made the wrong decision? He had been so sure God was leading him to do something that would make a bigger impact for the kingdom. He grew more and more depressed about his circumstances.

One day, Jeff hit rock bottom. He couldn't even get out of bed. He didn't recognize the enemy was trying to sabotage his spiritual effectiveness. But God knew just what Jeff needed. He drew four men to stand with Jeff—friends who deeply loved him and were committed to helping him endure and grow during that faith-stretching season. This band of brothers spent time listening, encouraging, and challenging Jeff to get back with God and start taking action with his life again.

If those four guys had not rallied around Jeff during that dark hour, he may not be where he is today with God—fully surrendered and serving others through various opportunities that maximize his S.H.A.P.E.

Jeff's story reminds us of a very important truth: You were not meant to go through life alone. You need people in your life to help you find and fulfill your Kingdom Purpose.

Who in your life can you request help from at any given time? Is there a friend, a spouse, a pastor? Maybe a counselor, a coach, one of your neighbors, or a small group member? Perhaps you have a mentor with whom you share the details of your life. The bottom line is that you need people in your life who can support you. We all do. As the poet John Donne wrote, "No man is an island." God built us—custom-designed us—to live best in Spirit-filled community.

Notice I did not say "superficial community." Far too often, we tend to settle for shallow relationships because they are easier. We don't have to invest as much time in them. And until we experience true community with others, we won't see the benefits offered by these deeper connections.

Deeper relationships are significant because they are Spirit-led, caring, authentic, challenging, supportive, and transparent. When we engage in superficial relationships, we tend to downplay the negative emotions we are feeling. When others ask us how we are doing, we say, "just fine," to avoid appearing weak or needy. Our society reveres independence – usually to its own hurt.

"Just fine." My friend Frank once told me that FINE stands for "Feelings Inside Never Expressed." I can't count the number of times I've answered, "I'm fine," when in reality I'm anything *but* fine. I simply don't want to burden anyone with my "stuff." Holding back like that robs me – as well as my friends – of the blessings that can only be experienced when we allow others to support us. I'm not suggesting you unload your emotional baggage on the grocery store checker or the parking attendant. I'm talking about being honest with the significant people in your life – the people you love and who love you in return.

During our first few years of marriage, my wife would ask, "How was your day?" when I came home from work. I consistently responded with the familiar but emotionless, "Fine." Through her patient encouragement, I eventually learned that letting her and others into my life is extremely rewarding. When we choose to have significant relationships, "I'm fine" turns into "I could be better," "I'm hurting," or even "I'm great!"

Building significant relationships is simply not optional. It is part of the law of Christ. The Bible says, "Share each other's troubles and problems, and in this way obey the law of Christ" (Galatians 6:2, NLT). You and I must request help from others so we can fully become who God made us to be and have an opportunity to do the unique work he has planned for us.

It All Starts with Love

The foundation of the Christian life *must* be love. If *love* is not at the center of our relationships, they will never open the door to discover the worth and meaning God has in store for us.

When several teachers challenged Jesus to summarize all the commandments in the Bible, he answered by saying the first and greatest command is to "'Love the Lord your God with all your heart and with all your soul and with all your mind and with all your strength.' The second [command] is this: 'Love your neighbor as yourself.' There is no commandment greater than these" (Mark 12:30–31).

As we fall more deeply in love with God and with the person he has made us to be, our love for him will inevitably spill over to others. People who have experienced God's transforming love reciprocate by showering others with God-motivated love. The Bible says, "Dear friends, since God so loved us, we also ought to love one another. No one has ever seen God; but if we love one another, God lives in us and his love is made complete in us" (1 John 4:11–12). Just as with building significant relationships, loving others and allowing them to love us is not optional for those who claim to be followers of Jesus Christ.

It has taken me years to grasp the concept of love. What most of us view as traditional love commonly enters our lives when we are children. Godly parents have a responsibility to model Christlike love to their children as a strong and secure foundation to build upon as they grow. Those who, like me, have experienced emotional or physical abandonment by parents, however, need to realize that we may not have such a foundation to build upon. Maybe your idea of love has been formed by broken relationships, self-help books, counselors, or the media. It is imperative that your concept of love reflect Christ. If it doesn't, you must create a *new* model of love that originates from him.

I had to find this Christlike model of love before I could really mature in life. Today, I'm able to accept and appreciate love from others. I'm grateful to my wife who is the most forgiving, patient, loving, caring person I have ever known. I'm also thankful for the people in my life who continually give me grace as I continue to increase my capacity to love and be loved.

I encourage you to be sure that your model of love is a reflection of God's grace, so you can truly immerse yourself in the abundant rewards of relationships centered in love. The Bible says, "And now these three remain: faith, hope and love. But the greatest of these is love" (1 Corinthians 13:13).

Rewards of Love

Having relationships driven by love bring countless rewards to life. An entire section in the New Testament – the "love chapter," 1 Corinthians

13 – is devoted to the topic. I have quoted this passage at many weddings and heard it read at my own. The rewards of loving relationships mentioned in that chapter, however, go far beyond the marital union. The writer, the apostle Paul, addresses everyone – from the church at Corinth to readers today – about love at every level of our lives.

Look at what Paul says about the characteristics and rewards of love: "Love is patient, love is kind. It does not envy, it does not boast, it is not proud. It is not rude, it is not self-seeking, it is not easily angered, it keeps no record of wrongs. Love does not delight in evil but rejoices with the truth. It always protects, always trusts, always hopes, always perseveres" (vv. 4 – 7).

Consider whether or not you could benefit from having a group of people in your life who …

- Are patient with you
- Treat you with kindness
- You do not need to compete with
- Are not boastful
- Are more proud of you than of themselves
- Are not rude to you
- Are not easily angered by your actions
- Do not hold your past against you
- Help you live by the truth of God's Word

What a wonderful list of rewards for simply allowing people into our lives! I'm so grateful God has given me everything on that list through my relationships with other believers. I don't deserve any of it. I thank God for every person. They are in my life by the inexpressible grace of God.

Have you been blessed like that through specific people in your life?

God's Word says, "Accept one another, then, just as Christ accepted you, in order to bring praise to God" (Romans 15:7). The blessing comes with the complete acceptance, affirmation, and appreciation we receive from those we are in relationship with. The author of the book of Hebrews urges us to "encourage one another daily, as long as it is called Today, so that none of you may be hardened by sin's deceitfulness" (Hebrews 3:13).

The believers God has drawn around me encourage me and confront me in love when I'm meandering off course in my spiritual walk. I can't recommend this highly enough. It's almost as though I have a personal cheerleading team constantly feeding me "verbal vitamins"—the words of encouragement and challenge I need as I strive to live with and for God.

Our plan is to do life together. We have no intention to stop meeting; our goal is to remain present in each other's lives. God's Word says, "And let us consider how we may spur one another on toward love and good deeds. Let us not give up meeting together, as some are in the habit of doing, but let us encourage one another—and all the more as you see the Day approaching" (Hebrews 10:24–25).

Ears to Hear

God gave us ears because he knew we would need them to navigate life. When we hear the sound of sirens behind us, we know to pull our car over to the side of the road. When a doorbell rings, we know it means someone is at the front door. Today, most of us have even learned to distinguish the sound of our own cell phone in a crowded room. Our brains can process the thousands, if not millions, of sounds our ears perceive.

I have learned to listen to and adjust my life by one sound in partic- ular—the sound of godly advice. If you and I are going to become the masterpieces God wants to make of us, we must have ears to hear the wisdom God chooses to speak through the people around us. The Bible says, "Above all and before all, do this: Get Wisdom! Write this at the top of your list: Get Understanding!" (Proverbs 4:7, MSG).

One way to get this wisdom is through the Word of God. Another important way is through the godly counsel of others.

For years, I thought God was going to use me to speak to thousands in stadium events so I could help mobilize the masses for him. I imag- ined myself with exactly the right combination of spiritual gifts needed to accomplish this vision. I shared my dream with a mentor of mine when we met for coffee one morning.

As I was outlining all these plans, my friend stopped me. "Erik," he said, "I believe God loves you and has a great plan for your life, but this is not part of it right now."

I couldn't quite believe my ears. How could this wise man doubt God's plan? He went on to ask, "Can you point to one time over the past five years that God has opened doors that would support this dream?" I was stunned. He was right! I could not point to a single instance. My friend then said, "Erik, could you be wanting this dream to meet some of your emotional insecurities, caused by the abandonment of your earthly father?"

He might as well have said, "Checkmate." I realized he was absolutely right. You probably could have heard the air whistling out of my balloon. God used this wise and faithful man to give me advice that, at the time, was difficult to hear.

As I look back on it now, I can genuinely thank him for daring to share his heart in that situation. Now I know to take my dreams and desires to my life support team for review before I become emotionally attached to them. I recommend it for everyone – it saves a lot of soul-searching later on. My close friends encourage some of my hopes and dreams. Some dreams they challenge me to take even further, as they did with my dream of writing this book.

Please be willing to hear the wisdom God gives you through your significant relationships. Be willing to change your course when God speaks to you through them. By doing so, you will be able to discern what is worth your spiritual and emotional investment – the visions that honor God, rather than desires that benefit only you.

S.H.A.P.E. Training Team

In medical emergency situations, a person can be saved by a life support system that provides the oxygen needed to survive. In much the same way, you need a *relational* life support system to provide you with the essential care, love, and encouragement – your spiritual oxygen – so you are able to survive and thrive for Jesus.

My goal for the remainder of this chapter is to help you start building your own S.H.A.P.E. Training Team.

I must admit, I wasn't very excited when a close friend first introduced me to this concept. I thought to myself, *Why do I need people in my life? Asking people for help is a sign of weakness. I can do it on my own.*

Up until then, I hadn't experienced many good relationships. Over the years, I gradually realized that the "father of lies" wanted me to think

I could do this whole *life* thing by myself. I'm thankful for the way my life changed once I acknowledged my need for a team to care for me, champion me, and challenge me. I never would have imagined that allowing people into my life and letting them love me fully would bring such release and replenishment to my spirit. God wants to meet our deepest needs through relationships.

As you prepare to assemble your own S.H.A.P.E. Training Team, keep two key character qualities in mind.

First, seriously consider making it a prerequisite that team members are devoted to Jesus Christ. If you are going to maximize your God-given S.H.A.P.E. and make a significant contribution with your life, your team must be "believer based."

Second, select only team members whose core values match your own. These people will significantly influence your life—for good or bad. So invite in only people who are dedicated to God; strive to live surrendered lives; pay attention to others; show true love toward others; have a humble spirit; and desire to use their resouces to help others. You will find that the people who demonstrate these qualities will have a lasting, positive influence on you.

I'm not suggesting, of course, that you close yourself off to relationships with nonbelievers. That would be tragic, since Christ has called us to be salt and light in this world. But you wouldn't hire a hair stylist to fix your computer, would you? If you went to the gym, you'd want a qualified personal trainer to help you meet your training goals. The same is true when it comes to those who will be directly impacting your personal spiritual growth. You need Christlike people to nurture Christlikeness in your life.

My own S.H.A.P.E. Training Team is made up of three components: my Training Partner, my Training Group, and my Board of Advisors.

If you wonder why I use the word *training* within these three areas of my team, it's for a very important reason. The Bible places an emphasis on training ourselves to be who God made us to be. The apostle Paul even talked about it as a way he was going to live his life: "So I run straight to the goal with purpose in every step. I am not like a boxer who misses his punches. I discipline my body like an athlete, *training* it to do what it should" (1 Corinthians 9:26–27, NLT, italics added). Paul also wrote,

"Have nothing to do with godless myths and old wives' tales; rather, *train* yourself to be godly. For physical training is of some value, but godliness has value for all things, holding promise for both the present life and the life to come" (1 Timothy 4:7–8, italics added).

I love what John Ortberg says in his book, *The Life You've Always Wanted*, when it comes to training ourselves, "Spiritual transformation is not a matter of trying harder, but of training wiser." Trying to live for Jesus doesn't work, but training ourselves does, which is why we need a team of people around us to help.

Let's unpack each of these vital roles to help you consider who you will ask to join your team.

Your Training Partner

Your Training Partner will become your weekly – even daily – source of support, prayer, encouragement, and correction. Your partner must be someone you feel certain you can trust, someone you know you could go the distance with – a close friend or, if you are married, perhaps your spouse.

Training Partners typically are in your same season of life and have similar life goals. My Training Partner is my best friend. Although we have very different careers (he is a corporate executive, and I'm a pastor), we have a lot in common. We enjoy many of the same things. We are close in age. Our kids are all within a few years of each other. Our wives are close friends as well. Even though our strengths and passions don't parallel, we both genuinely want to help the other go the distance for God and remain faithful to who he has made us to be.

One aspect of this relationship that makes it work is that we do not compete with each other. We have discovered that when competition between us decreases, our connection with one another increases. We are both very competitive individuals, especially on the basketball court, but when it comes to life – the things that go deeper than hobbies or social events – competition has no place in our relationship. We are completely free to be one another's cheerleaders on the playing court of life.

I ask my Training Partner to focus primarily on the condition of my heart, because my heart reveals the real me. I need someone checking my motives on a regular basis. I also need a safe place to confess my sins. In the book of James we are told, "Make this your common practice: Confess your sins to each other and pray for each other so that you can live together whole and healed. The prayer of a person living right with God is something powerful to be reckoned with" (James 5:16, MSG).

As my Training Partner, my friend challenges my private thought life, my character, the condition of my soul, my core values, and helps me make course corrections as I strive to fulfill what I feel God is clearly asking me to do for him.

He helps me wrestle with those areas where the enemy tries hardest to take me down. It is vital for me, as it is for anyone who strives to live for God, to have a place to confess my struggles and share my life situations and successes, knowing I will not be judged, but loved and encouraged.

Do you have this type of relationship in your life? Is there anyone who stands apart as someone you want to rely on in this way? If not, ask God to help you develop such a relationship. Maybe someone already is filling this role in your life, but you haven't recognized it before now. Who is it? If so, contact this special person and tell them how much you appreciate them being in your life.

Your Training Group

As valuable as a Training Partner is, having others to stand beside you is even better. The Bible says, "By yourself you're unprotected. With a friend you can face the worst. Can you round up a third? A three-stranded rope isn't easily snapped" (Ecclesiastes 4:12, MSG).

A Training Group typically is made up of friends or peers who have bonded with each other, people who are committed to going the distance with each other. Again, your Training Group members should have similar core values and a longing to be part of a team whose goal is to post wins for God. Your Training Partner can be a part of your Training Group.

My Training Group consists of ten members. These wonderful people meet with me on a regular basis for coaching and care. We are committed to helping each other handle life and all that it offers. We pray for each other, encourage each other, and hold each other accountable. We cheer each other on in doing the work God has specifically planned for us. Simply put, we *do life together*.

God's Word reveals the secret to making it work: "You can develop a healthy, robust community that lives right with God and enjoy its results *only* if you do the hard work of getting along with each other, treating each other with dignity and honor" (James 3:18, MSG, italics added).

The gospel of Luke tells a story which perfectly describes the traits of a Training Group:

> Some men came carrying a paralytic on a mat and tried to take him into the house to lay him before Jesus. When they could not find a way to do this because of the crowd, they went up on the roof and lowered him on his mat through the tiles into the middle of the crowd, right in front of Jesus. When Jesus saw their faith, he said, "Friend, your sins are forgiven" (Luke 5:18–20).

This story shows us three kinds of people: the Healer, Jesus; the Hurting, the man who needed to be healed; and the Helpers, the paralyzed man's team of friends—his Training Group, if you will. This dedicated group of men showed tremendous resolve as they fought for their friend to be seen by Jesus. It was their faith that put him in a position to be healed by Jesus. Imagine being that paralytic man. He'd lived like that for years, and likely experienced recurring dreams in which he walked, ran, danced, and enjoyed life like everyone else. You could say his loyal friends were his own personal "dream team," because they helped make his dream come true.

When life is tough and you don't feel you have the energy to even go to Jesus in prayer, do you have a team of people who can intercede on your behalf? Do you have a S.H.A.P.E. Training Group? If you are going to maximize your S.H.A.P.E. and make a significant contribution with your life for God, I urge you to be about building such a team now, before another day goes by.

Your Board of Advisors

Beyond a Training Partner and a Training Group, I also have what I refer to as my personal Board of Advisors. This group is made up of seasoned mentors who are sources of wisdom during those seasons of life in which I need greater clarity. In addition, I seek these key people out to help sharpen and strengthen my S.H.A.P.E. Sometimes we'll meet in person, sometimes on the phone; sometimes we use email; sometimes I just read their wisdom in books.

For example, when it comes to management and leadership advice, I seek the written wisdom of the late Peter Drucker. When it comes to raising my kids, I look to experts like John Townsend and Henry Cloud. When it comes to honoring my wife, I seek the help of Gary Smalley, author of several books on relationship success.

My friend Mark is an expert when it comes to using his Board of Advisors. Mark and his wife and kids are part of our church family at Saddleback Church. As a businessman, Mark oversees a division of his company that does well over $100 million in annual sales. When I asked Mark, "What keeps you focused?" he answered, "God, my family, and my monthly group gathering with my advisors." Mark's team is made up of Christ-centered business owners who share similar success.

"We meet each month to support and keep each other accountable," Mark told me. "We focus not only on business, but also on our families. We talk about how to live a significant life for Jesus. We challenge each other to make positive changes in our personal, professional, and family lives."

As you think about your personal Board of Advisors, imagine sitting at a boardroom table with empty chairs. Who would you want to invite to fill those chairs and sit at the table with you? Who would you want investing in you? Who are the role models, encouragers, sources of wis-

Jesus
CEO

My Board of Advisors

dom and knowledge you can learn from? On the diagram at the bottom of page 156, place next to each chair the name and area of life in which you see each person helping you. You will notice your CEO has already been named.

Pray, Then Pursue

Now that you have been introduced to the key elements of your S.H.A.P.E. Training Team—your Training Partner, your Training Group, and your Board of Advisors—let's examine how you may want to build your team.

In building my own, I used a practical but powerful model from the Bible: I copied Jesus.

I looked at the story of how Jesus appointed his twelve disciples—his life support team—in Luke 6:12–13: "Jesus went out to a mountainside to pray, and spent the night praying to God. When morning came, he called his disciples to him and chose twelve of them." Jesus gives us two essential principles for inviting others into our lives: Pray and Pursue.

First, Jesus *prayed.* The Bible says he prayed all night to God the Father. Can you imagine praying all night—for eight hours straight? Sometimes I have a hard time focusing for eight minutes! Why do you think Jesus did this? I believe it was because he knew he needed help fulfilling his mission on earth, and his Father's wisdom to identify his top twelve recruits. With a decision that important, he would not have just put names in a hat and said, "Okay, the first twelve names I pick will make up my team."

If Jesus needed the Father's help in picking his disciples, how much more do you and I need help in selecting the members of our S.H.A.P.E. Training Team? We are in a spiritual battle. Satan does not want us to have a S.H.A.P.E. Training Team. His goal is to see us fall, and he knows that's exactly what will happen if we try to live the Christian life alone.

Second, Jesus *passionately pursued* the team members God revealed to him. Jesus did not wait for his disciples to come to him; he went after them. The Bible says he *called* them. He pursued them proactively. Such pursuit shows he cared for them and longed for them to be with him. It also reveals his knowledge of their strengths, and how he wanted to steer them in ways they could express these strengths for the sake of the gospel.

Requesting help from others may seem impossible to you, but God asks us to take the risk. Peter didn't have the amazing experience of walking on water until he stepped out of the storm-tossed boat. Let God make the impossible possible in your life.

Tell Them You Love Them

Every summer for several years now, certain members of my S.H.A.P.E. Training Team spend a week at Forest Home Family Camp in the San Bernardino Mountains. Our five families have grown to love this annual adventure, sharing a week of fun, good food, and great fellowship.

The week ends on Friday morning at the "Victory Circle," a treasured tradition when as many as 150 families gather in this picturesque location, carved out of a mountain, for a final time of sharing. We claim victory for God, citing the great things he accomplished in each of us during the week.

I had a memorable experience in the Victory Circle on Friday, July 15, 2005.

The morning sun was streaming in through the large evergreen trees, and God nudged me to tell the entire group about a victory in my life. I took the microphone and told the group that standing in their midst reminded me of the circle of friends who had brought victory to my life. With tears streaming down my face, I looked at each of the couples who had come with us and thanked them for the difference they had made for me through their prayers, encouragement, support, and love. I thanked them for helping me be the husband and father God calls me to be and for allowing me to just be Erik, rather than "Pastor Erik," when I'm with them.

As I handed the microphone back to the camp leader, I noticed everyone else in my group was wiping tears from their eyes. We hugged and thanked God for each other.

I realized that was the first time in seven years I had made such a public declaration to these special people in my life. That day God reminded me that I need to deliberately make much more time to praise the people in my life. I need to tell them privately and publicly how thankful I am for each one of them.

Please don't wait seven years to tell your close community of friends how much you love them. Once you have assembled your S.H.A.P.E. Training Team, be sure to regularly take the time to celebrate each person who's part of it. Let them know now how much you need them and how much you love them.

Whoever you choose to be on your S.H.A.P.E. Training Team, do it with this in mind: your spiritual success in life depends largely on your relationships with others. Do you want to experience the best God has for the rest of your life? Begin by surrounding yourself with the best possible team—then get ready to make a significant difference!

GRABBING HOLD

As you close this chapter, spend some time asking God for the wisdom and strength you need to build your S.H.A.P.E. Training Team. Ask him to help you experience true community and all the rewards that come with it.

■ ■ ■ ■ ■

Reflect on what you have learned. What are a few things you learned from this chapter about the importance of having godly relationships?

Realize what you have been given. Below, write a thank-you note to God for one person who recently has helped you in a time of need. Then write a thank-you note to that person.

Request help from others. Who are two models of faith that inspire you? How can you learn from them?

Respond in faith. Who will you pray for and pursue to be on your life support team?

Who will be your Training Partner? Maybe you already have a Training Partner. If so, use this as a reminder to thank him or her for making a difference in your life. If you don't currently have a Training Partner, begin praying for one and, when the time comes, pursue them proactively and passionately.

I will begin praying for _____

who I will ask to be my Training Partner.

Who will be part of your Training Group? Think of four or five people you could invite to be part of your Training Group. List your reasons for selecting these particular individuals. How will these people enhance your life? What are their core values? How can *you* help *them*?

Who will you appoint to your Board of Advisors? List the people you could invite to be your Board of Advisors. Why would you appoint these specific individuals? How will they influence you? How will these people help you remain faithful to who God has made you to be?

Unleashing Your S.H.A.P.E. for Life

Chapter 10

KINGDOM PURPOSE

Grasping your Unique Assignment from God

Commit to the LORD whatever you do,
and your plans will succeed.
Proverbs 16:3

Serving is the pathway to real significance.
Rick Warren

God can do amazing things with us
when we desire to say "yes" to him.
Denny Bellesi

You were made to make a significant difference.

Steve sat staring at those eight words written on the whiteboard in my office. The sun's light only exaggerated the tears that flowed too freely down his face. He longed to redirect his life, to grasp his specific life purpose, to make a significant kingdom difference. But the starting point for this change was not showing itself.

Steve said to me, "Erik, how do I move from knowing my S.H.A.P.E. to fulfilling my Kingdom Purpose?"

It's a question I had heard many times over. I told Steve that he had reached the summit of his discovery journey with God. Just like climbing to the top of a mountain allows a person to gain a new view of their surroundings, Steve now had a new view of his life—just as you do at this point—but how was he to proceed with this fresh perspective of himself?

I decided to show him a video clip from the movie *Chariots of Fire* that provides some insight.

In this famous film, runners Eric Liddell and Harold Abrahams represent Britain in the 400-meter sprint at the 1924 Olympic games. On the day of the big race, Eric, a committed Christian, is handed a scrap of paper from a fellow athlete, with 1 Samuel 2:30 written on it: "He who honors me, I will honor." Clutching the paper tightly in his fist, he later sprints toward the finish line, about to win the gold medal. As the camera closes in on his tense, sweaty face, the viewer hears Eric's now-famous words: "God made me fast, and when I run, I feel his pleasure."

This was Eric Liddell's Kingdom Purpose. Although I'm sure there were many other things at which he excelled, there was one thing that allowed him to feel God's pleasure like nothing else—running fast. If you were to watch the entire movie you would see that he uses this unique purpose to bring God glory.

After we watched that clip, I wrote another sentence on my whiteboard for Steve:

God made me _____ and when I _____ I feel his pleasure.
Your S.H.A.P.E.   Your Purpose

I asked Steve if he could fill in the first blank. That wasn't hard for him, having spent a lot of time recently discovering his unique S.H.A.P.E. But the second blank still had him stumped.

I then read Psalm 119:31–32 to Steve: "I hold fast to your statutes, O LORD; do not let me be put to shame. I run in the path of your commands, for you have set my heart free."

Steve said to me, "I only want to run the path God has for me. I'm tired of all the other paths that I have tried and left me feeling empty. I truly want my heart set free to focus only on what God has for me."

So I told Steve that if he truly wanted to grasp his specific Kingdom Purpose, he would need to take five sequential steps as he started his descent down the mountain with God. I also told Steve he needed to hold his Kingdom Purpose lightly and thankfully, giving God all of the glory. To make sure this happened, I told him to always make God the hero of everything he does from this day forward. As Rick Warren says, "It's not about you."

The goal of this chapter is helping you take the same five steps Steve took many years ago, so that you too can grasp your specific Kingdom Purpose and begin fulfilling it for God's glory. Here are those steps, in an acrostic that spells GRASP for easy recall:

1. **G**et with God. As we have learned, apart from God we can't achieve anything of lasting significance. So the first step toward grasping your Kingdom Purpose is to make sure God is not just in your life, but at the center of it. This is why you spent time letting go of the stuff that has been distracting you and weighing you down.

2. **R**ealize your Kingdom Dream. Once God has his rightful place as the pilot of your life, let your heart and mind start dreaming for his kingdom. Let the quiet whispers of your heart ring loud for God's glory.

3. **A**ctivate your Serving Sweet Spot. This is the optimal zone of your life where your S.H.A.P.E. is best expressed. It is at this step that you start to align your God-given uniqueness with your God-honoring dream, which leads to securing your unique Kingdom Purpose.

4. **S**eek wisdom. The fourth step is all about confirmation and support. It is at this point that you share your Kingdom Purpose

with members of your S.H.A.P.E. Training Team and ask for honest feedback before starting to alter your schedule to fulfill your purpose.

5. **P**lan your test-drive. The final step to grasping your Kingdom Purpose is to try it out. All your time and energy now converges into an action plan. This is not a self-help plan, but a Spirit-guided map that keeps you on course with God's calling on your life.

Now we will explore each of these steps in greater detail and apply them to your life.

Step #1: Get with God

As you have discovered, God is the author of your life and wants you to honor him with it. We can't grasp what God has for us unless we are dedicated to loving him the way he loves us—with all our heart, soul, mind, and strength. When we love God this way, our motives are Spirit-filled and we focus on serving others. When we don't, our motives are selfish and we focus only on serving ourselves. As you prepare to GRASP your Kingdom Purpose, make sure your connection with God is clog-free.

Jesus drew a word picture of this concept when he said, "I am the vine; you are the branches. Those who remain in me, and I in them, will produce much fruit. For apart from me you can do nothing" (John 15:5, NLT). He makes it crystal clear that our choice is between connecting with God and being fruitful, or not connecting and doing nothing of eternal significance with our lives. Do you want to be fruitful, or do you want to do nothing?

I confess I have a tendency to run ahead of God, but the truth is, we can't bypass God. We must spend time with him so he can teach us to trust him with everything. We must immerse ourselves in God's Word and allow him to speak to us through it. We must spend time communing with him in prayer—not just *talking* to him, but *listening* to what he has to say to us.

The Bible says, "Trust in the LORD with all your heart and lean not on your own understanding; in all your ways acknowledge him, and he will make your paths straight" (Proverbs 3:5–6). As you trust God more, continuing to release your life to him, he will reveal what he has for you and you will be able to grasp that wisdom—no matter what your past has been like.

This reminds me of a note I got from Patty, a participant at a S.H.A.P.E. seminar. She wrote:

> I know we are only one week into this discovery process, but already I'm feeling a sense of panic rising from my depths. I seriously struggle with a performance-based, shame-filled past that has driven me to be a huge people pleaser most of my life. I'm fifty-one years old. I've raised three beautiful children. My husband divorced me three years ago, after eighteen years of struggling in a very difficult marriage. I've attended church off and on for over twelve years (more off than on). I've been through twelve years of therapy to heal from a very difficult past, and through it all have remained a deeply faithful individual.
>
> Right now I am very alone. No, I am not a member of a small group for several reasons; I think the most foundational one is that I'm terrified. Except for my kids, who I see at least once or twice each week, and a couple of people I bump into because of other activities in my life, I am really alone.
>
> I signed up for your seminar because I honestly do not know what to do with the rest of my life. Mostly it feels pointless, directionless, and awfully lonely. I tried to do the homework, and I just can't come up with any answers. I have never felt so lost in my life....
>
> I don't exactly know what I want. Prayers for clearer direction and peace would be nice. An email from God would help, but I'm not holding my breath on that one! I guess I just need some encouragement—maybe someone to tell me that taking time off from being productive and coming to a dead stop after racing through life at 150 mph for fifty-some-odd years is an okay thing to do.

I encouraged Patty that God was at work in her circumstances—as difficult as they were—to prepare her for the Kingdom Purpose he had planned for her to fulfill. I suggested that the best things she could do was to get with God and give herself permission to be who God made her to be—so she could start taking hold of what God had for her. As I write this, she is starting to grasp her specific Kingdom Purpose—because she made a strong connection with God.

A strong connection with God is essential if we are to experience everything he has in store for us. That is why in chapter seven I asked you to inventory your life so you could surrender the things that were distracting you and slowing you down from fulfilling your Kingdom Purpose.

The Bible says, "We are confident of all this because of our great trust in God through Christ. It is not that we think we can do anything of lasting value by ourselves. Our only power and success come from God" (2 Corinthians 3:4–5, NLT). Just like Patty, you need to be real and vulnerable with God about your life. He knows everything, but wants you to take the time to tell him about your frustrations and failures and whatever sin clogs your connection with him and distances you from his power.

The fact is, all of us have sinned and distanced ourselves from God. The key is to admit to God that we have missed his target for our lives. "If we confess our sins, he is faithful and just and will forgive us our sins and purify us from all unrighteousness" (1 John 1:9). When we confess, God graciously wipes our slate clean, even though we don't deserve it on our own. He forgives us because Jesus himself has already paid the price for our sin.

After David had committed adultery with Bathsheba, he cried out, "Have mercy on me, O God, according to your unfailing love; according to your great compassion blot out my transgressions. Wash away all my iniquity and cleanse me from my sin" (Psalm 51:1–2). Whatever sins you have committed, large or small, God wants you to confess them to him so your connection with him is clear. Is there anything in your life you need to confess to God so you can be right with him? If so, do it now.

After you have gotten matters straight with God, celebrate his goodness! The apostle Paul urges us: "Rejoice in the Lord always. I will say it again: Rejoice!" (Philippians 4:4). When I spend time with God, I like to start by rejoicing in his grace and goodness. I want him to know how much I appreciate all the blessings he has poured out in my life.

This is a good time for you to celebrate God in your life. Take a few minutes to write out a "brag-a-mony"—bragging on God for all he has done and is doing in your life.

God, thank you for ...

Step #2: Realize Your Kingdom Dream

Now that your connection with God is consistent and clear, the second step is realizing your Kingdom Dream. It all starts with a dream.

On August 28, 1963, standing on the steps at the Lincoln Memorial in Washington D.C., Martin Luther King Jr. delivered his famous "I have a dream" speech. That dream changed a man, who changed a city, which changed a state, which changed a nation. All these amazing things began with an ordinary man who was connected to God and who allowed God's voice to lead him. God wants to do the same with you. Your Kingdom Dream is the foundation of your Kingdom Purpose.

Are you living your Kingdom Dream, or are you just living? Bruce Wilkinson says in his book, *The Dream Giver*, "No matter where I travel in the world—whether among hard-charging Manhattan urbanites or villagers in South Africa—I have yet to find a person who didn't have a dream. They may not be able to describe it. They may have forgotten it. They may no longer believe in it. But it's there."

I could line up hundreds of people who feel they have a dream deep inside of them. It may be so deep inside that it's actually buried, but, as Wilkinson said, "it's there." Some people are afraid to accept their dream, scared to fulfill it. Others are eager to seize it. God wants us to seize it. Once we do, he can expand it to be everything he wants it to be.

And God's Dream for you is far more wonderful than you realize. The Bible says that God "is able to do far more than we would ever dare to ask or even dream of—infinitely beyond our highest prayers, desires, thoughts, or hopes" (Ephesians 3:20, TLB).

When you truly grasp what this verse is saying, you will be awed to the point of speechless gratitude. God is shouting at us: "Dream big! Think out of the box! Come up with the largest Kingdom Dream you can, and I will multiply it far beyond your wildest imagination!" God's plan and desire is to produce an amazingly abundant harvest of fruit from your little tree. It is up to you, however, to give his vision room to grow.

It seems every significant accomplishment for God starts off as an idea in one person's mind—a dream, a vision, or a goal.

In his book, *Good to Great*, Jim Collins challenges his readers to set a BHAG—a "Big Hairy Audacious Goal." Jim writes:

> A BHAG engages people—it reaches out and grabs them in the gut. It is tangible, energizing, highly focused. People "get it" right away; it takes little or no explanation. For example, the 1960s moon mission didn't need a committee to spend endless hours wordsmithing the goal into a verbose, impossible-to-remember "mission statement." The goal itself—the mountain to climb—was so easy to grasp, so compelling in its own right, that it could be said one hundred different ways, yet be easily understood by everyone. When an expedition sets out to climb Mount Everest, it doesn't need a three-page mission statement to explain what Mount Everest is. Most corporate statements we've seen do little to provoke forward movement because they do not contain the powerful mechanism of a BHAG.

Catching a God-sized vision gives the Lord an opportunity to do something amazing in you and through you.

Chip Ingram outlines what a God-sized vision is in his book, *Holy Ambition*:

> Vision is getting the big picture. Vision is a God-given burden to see what a person, a place or a situation could become if the grace of God and the power of God were unleashed on them. That's all a vision is. It doesn't mean your brain works differently from other people. It just means that something happens inside of you and you see things differently. Vision most often crystallizes around some burden or need, and as a result you see single moms or abused kids or a workplace situation or something in your home that needs to be and can be

changed. Vision goes right by the "how" for a moment and sees the goal accomplished. That's vision!

"We can see how this worked in Nehemiah's life," Chip continues. "When Nehemiah prayed, he asked God, 'What do you want me to do?' You don't just jump out and do something foolish. You get a word from God. You claim promises from Scriptures. You let God work in you."

Chip concludes, "Chapter 1 of Nehemiah begins with an individual. All great movements do. When God does something great, He starts with one person who has an idea, a dream, a vision. So the real question isn't, 'What can one person do?' but 'Am I willing to be the one person God uses to make a difference in my world?'"

The Bible says, "Delight yourself in the LORD and he will give you the desires of your heart" (Psalm 37:4). When we get with God, our dreams and desires will be for him—that's why he grants them. Getting with God is not optional for someone who wants God's blessing over every area of life.

Your Kingdom Dream is your message to share with the world on the Master's behalf. Rick Warren calls it your "life message." He says:

> Your Life Message includes sharing your godly passions. God is a passionate God. He passionately *loves* some things and passionately *hates* other things. As you grow closer to him, he will give you a passion for something he cares about deeply so you can be a spokesman for him in the world. It may be a passion about a problem, a purpose, a principle, or a group of people. Whatever it is, you will feel compelled to speak up about it and do what you can to make a difference.

So the question becomes, **"What dream, vision, or message do you feel God nudging you to achieve for him that you couldn't fulfill without him?"**

Don't start worrying about your finances or your fears. Give yourself permission to dream risky dreams, because, as the Bible says, "What is impossible with men is possible with God" (Luke 18:27). If God is leading you to do something for him, don't you think he will take care of the details? Don't be distracted by the "problems." Your role is to seize the dream God has laid on your heart—and trust him to make the impossible possible. I encourage you to look back at your comments in chapter three ("Heart") as you reflect on this.

A word of caution: God does not define "big" the way most of us do. Society says big is about quantity – having the biggest title, the largest bank account, the biggest house. God, however, defines "big" by *quality*, not quantity. Quality is seen by God in our strong connection with him, our deep devotion to his purposes, our relentless faith, and our clear conviction to serve him in our generation.

The truth is, there is only one Mother Teresa, one Rick Warren, one Billy Graham. But there are millions of servants – people like you and me – created by God to fulfill their Kingdom Purpose through the expression of their unique S.H.A.P.E.

Have you ever taken the time to dream about how you could make the greatest impact for God with your life? Try it! You might find out that you fill up ten pages like John Baker did when he dreamed about Celebrate Recovery. Or it could be as simple as a single sentence. My personal Kingdom Dream is: *I dream that I would be used by God to empower every believer in the world to find and fulfill their unique Kingdom Purpose in life by embracing and expressing their S.H.A.P.E. for life.*

Maybe you would find it helpful to start by thinking of a few words to describe your dream, instead of a few pages or even a few sentences. Here is a list of phrases I have heard from people as they strive to make the greatest impact for God with their lives:

- I dream of funding kingdom initiatives that help people in poverty.
- I dream of leading and building teams for effective ministry.
- I dream about impacting children through music.
- I dream about creating beauty that draws people to Jesus.
- I dream about strengthening marriages from God's Word.
- I dream about educating people on how to live purposeful lives for God.
- I dream about launching and leading a church that reaches out to the emerging generation.
- I dream about harvesting souls for God.
- I dream about teaching Scripture to teenagers.
- I dream about igniting the kingdom passion of every young adult.
- I dream about unleashing the potential for God's work in the people around me.
- I dream about sharing God's love overseas.

- I dream about leveraging resources for kingdom growth.
- I dream about conquering world poverty for God.
- I dream about mentoring children who have been abused.
- I dream about managing people and processes for kingdom effectiveness.
- I dream about helping simplify lives with practical tools.
- I dream about restoring hope to hurting people.
- I dream about helping people overcome addictions with the love of Jesus.
- I dream about mentoring young women.
- I dream about meeting physical needs of those in financial difficulty.
- I dream about inspiring men to live godly lives.
- I dream about empowering people to live healthy lifestyles.
- I dream about developing tools that help people grow closer to God.
- I dream about writing stories that inspire teenagers to follow God.
- I dream about helping others grow spiritually.

As you give yourself permission to dream for the kingdom of God, don't worry about the size of your dream. Focus instead on its significance—serving God's people in your generation for his glory!

Now, put some pieces of your dream in writing. Remember, your dream is a picture of the future, something deep inside that you have longed to unleash for God's glory. You may even find it helpful to talk with members of your S.H.A.P.E. Training Team. Why not dream together for God?

I dream of the day that God would use me to make a significant contribution to his Kingdom by ...

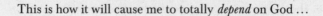

This is how it will cause me to totally *depend* on God ...

This is how it will totally *display* God's love toward others ...

Step #3: Activate Your Serving Sweet Spot

At this point, you have spent a lot of time assessing your God-given S.H.A.P.E. You have discovered what you are gifted to do, what you are passionate about, and what you naturally excel at doing. You have identified your personality style and realized that you have a wide array of experiences that can be used for God. Now it is time to put it all in the blender and see what God will make of it.

When you align your S.H.A.P.E. with your Kingdom Dream, you will be operating within your God-given Sweet Spot.

In the world of sports, the "sweet spot" is that place on a baseball bat, tennis racquet, or golf club that strikes the ball with maximum effectiveness and with little or no negative effect. Hitting the sweet spot is one reason athletes like Barry Bonds, Andre Agassi, and Tiger Woods swing so effortlessly, yet with such force.

God designed you with a Sweet Spot too. It's the area in which your S.H.A.P.E. is best expressed—typically recognized in those moments when others comment on your special ability to do something. When you operate in this area, you—like Bonds, Agassi, and Woods—are very effective and efficient. More important, when you are serving others within your Sweet Spot, you feel little or no negative force in your life because you are being true to who God made you to be.

The Bible says it this way:

> God has given each of us the ability to do certain things well. So if God has given you the ability to prophesy, speak out when you have faith that God is speaking through you. If your gift is that of serving others, serve them well. If you are a teacher, do a good job of teaching. If your gift is to encourage others, do it! If you have money, share it generously. If God has given you leadership ability, take the responsibility seriously. And if you have a gift for showing kindness to others, do it gladly (Romans 12:6–8, NLT).

Your Sweet Spot is located where the various parts of your S.H.A.P.E. (gifts, abilities, personality, and experiences) intersect with your Kingdom Dream (heart). This crossing of strengths and passions actually creates four quadrants, as shown in the following diagram. Each quadrant represents a key question for your life, the answers to which help you to start defining your unique Kingdom Purpose.

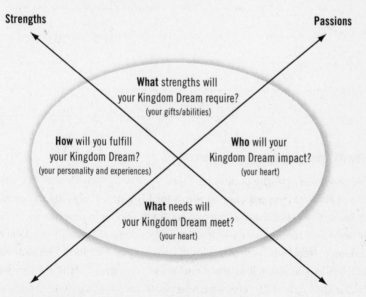

Let's explore each of these questions a bit further.

What Strengths Will Your Kingdom Dream Require?

There are certain things you love doing. They come so naturally, they don't seem like work at all. And the joy these tasks bring is all the reward you need. It might be something you do at work, but not necessarily. I have met people from many walks of life, and it's been my experience that few people get to express what they really love to do at their place of work.

Thankfully, God gave us all a contribution to make – regardless of what we do for a living. Whatever it is that you love to do, pursuing it will allow your passions to flow freely for God. He can use it all – from coaching to cooking, from leading to listening, from dancing to designing, from supervising to singing, from computing to counseling.

To help you assess you strengths, you may find it useful to look back at the Spiritual Gifts and Abilities sections of your S.H.A.P.E. *for* Life Profile (pp. 221, 222). Use what you wrote there to complete the following list.

Stepping out in faith with God to start fulfilling my Kingdom Dream will allow me to express the following spiritual gifts and abilities:

- _____
- _____
- _____
- _____
- _____

Who Will Your Kingdom Dream Impact?

Because God is in the people business, your Kingdom Dream will point to a specific target audience to touch for his glory. It may be the elderly or executives, children or caregivers, believers or nonbelievers, youth or young adults, men or women, leaders or loners. We all have a target audience. Who will your Kingdom Dream reach for God? You may find it helpful to look back at the Heart section of your S.H.A.P.E. *for* Life Profile (pp. 221 – 222). Use what you wrote there to complete the following list.

Stepping out in faith with God to start fulfilling my Kingdom Dream will allow me to reach out to and help the following people group(s):

- _____
- _____
- _____
- _____
- _____

What Needs Will Your Kingdom Dream Meet?

God wants us to use what he has given us to meet specific needs in the lives of others. The Bible says, "Praise be to the God and Father of our Lord Jesus Christ, the Father of compassion and the God of all comfort, who comforts us in all our troubles, so that we can comfort those in any trouble with the comfort we ourselves have received from God" (2 Corinthians 1:3–4).

Once you find your Sweet Spot and begin using your abilities for God's work, your biggest challenge likely will be reining yourself in. In your excitement, you will want to reach out in every direction to meet all kinds of needs. It's important to focus on those specific needs you feel God is asking *you* to meet—spiritual, relational, physical, emotional, educational, vocational, or other. Fortunately, God provides a gift of discernment that can help you identify them. If you do not have that gift yourself, find someone on your S.H.A.P.E. Training Team who does.

It's important to understand that there are different kinds of needs we meet as God's servants.

Some needs, for example, are *shared* needs—those we meet because we serve a loving Master. Jesus said, "And if anyone gives even a cup of cold water to one of these little ones because he is my disciple, I tell you the truth, he will certainly not lose his reward" (Matthew 10:42). *Specific* needs, on the other hand, are those we are personally passionate about meeting. You may find it helpful to look back at the Heart and Experiences sections of your S.H.A.P.E. *for* Life Profiles (pp. 221–223) in filling out this section. Use what you wrote there to respond to the following checklist:

Stepping out in faith with God to start fulfilling my Kingdom Dream will allow me to minister to others by meeting the following needs:

☐ Spiritual   ☐ Educational
☐ Relational   ☐ Vocational
☐ Physical   ☐ Other: _____
☐ Emotional

How Will You Fulfill Your Kingdom Dream?

God has inspired you with a Kingdom Dream that releases the things you love doing and meets the needs of the people he has put on your heart. The final thing you need to determine is how you will actually do it. It's important to identify the *services* you will provide and the *setting* in which you will deliver them. You will discover these two things through your strengths, personality, and experiences.

More specifically, revisit the positive portraits that you painted in chapter six. What are some experiences you found extremely rewarding and how might they help you better understand how you might express your Kingdom Dream? In addition, look back at how God has wired you to relate to others and respond to opportunities.

Your Services—These are the acts of loving service you will provide for your target group through the spiritual gifts and abilities you listed above. Now it's time to determine specifics. For example, if you selected teaching, what types of teaching will you offer? If you selected encouraging, how will you encourage? If you selected counseling, how will you do that and for whom? If you selected writing, what types will you offer?

Use the space below to brainstorm some specific ways to serve your target group.

- _____
- _____
- _____

- _____

- _____

*Your Setting—*Once you determine how your services can be used to help others, you need to decide the setting that will enable you to make the greatest impact. Some of us feel most comfortable working one-on-one; others work best in teams; still others enjoy the intensity of being "on stage."

Let's say, for example, that teaching is a service you will offer. You need to identify the best way for you to teach. The key here is to leverage your personality and experiences. If you have a proven track record of teaching from a platform, think of ways to use those experiences with your gifts and abilities to meet the needs of your target group.

Some personalities are best suited to serving God in smaller settings, such as one-on-one or small groups. I can't stress enough the importance of knowing yourself in order to make these key decisions about your future. God knows you best, so listen to him. Get to know when it's really him tapping you on the heart, as opposed to your own desires.

It may be helpful to review the Personality and Experiences sections of your S.H.A.P.E. *for* Life Profile (pp. 222–223) at this time. Use what you wrote there to complete the following list.

I feel the best setting for me to start expressing my Kingdom Dream is:

- _____

- _____

- _____

- _____

- _____

Your Kingdom Purpose Statement

Remember Steve from the beginning of this chapter and the sentence that I asked him to complete on my office whiteboard? After a few months of prayer and trying out various service opportunities, he was able to fine-tune his "Kingdom Purpose Statement."

He wrote, *God made me* ... a driven leader and consultant totally focused on sharing his love with corporate executives ... *and when I* ... help them improve their communication/presentation skills, God opens doors for me to share my testimony and when I do ... *I feel his pleasure.*

As you can see, Steve has the gift of leadership, the natural abilities of coaching and consulting, and a passion to impact corporate executives; he desires variety, is people oriented, and wants to help others both vocationally and spiritually. All of this came from Steve's Sweet Spot. In addition, it totally aligns with and helps advance his Kingdom Dream of sharing God's love with as many people as possible within corporate America.

Now it's your turn. Given all you have learned in this book, and having completed the preceding exercises in this chapter, has God graciously allowed you to start defining your Kingdom Purpose? Could you fill in those two blanks in that sentence? Summarize, in the space below, who God has created you to be and what he is calling you to do on his behalf.

God made me ...

and when I ...

I feel his pleasure.

What you have just written is a draft of your unique Kingdom Purpose! How does your Kingdom Purpose Statement align with and help advance your Kingdom Dream? This is a good question to answer with some of the key people from your S.H.A.P.E. Training Team. As you seek help and wisdom from others and experiment in various areas of ministry, you will inevitably refine this statement about your life. As I think about it, mine has probably had hundreds of alterations in the years as I have journeyed with God.

Now that you have taken the time to craft your Serving Sweet Spot, clarify your findings by taking the *Your Serving Sweet Spot Assessment* online at *www.shapediscovery .com*. Just use the unique access code printed on the inside of the book jacket to take advantage of this great tool. Once you have finished the assessment, you will receive a customized *Your Serving Sweet Spot Profile* that you can share with members of your S.H.A.P.E. Training Team as you seek their wisdom. Have fun!

Step #4: Seek Wisdom

In order to start faithfully expressing your Kingdom Purpose and fulfilling your Kingdom Dream, you will need people in your life to cheer for you, challenge you, and counsel you. The Bible talks about each of these roles.

The writer of Hebrews tells us to cheer for each other: "But encourage one another daily, as long as it is called Today, so that none of you may be hardened by sin's deceitfulness" (Hebrews 3:13).

The book of Proverbs tells us to give others permission to challenge us: "As iron sharpens iron, a friend sharpens a friend" (Proverbs 27:17, NLT).

And you will need wise counsel to keep on track. The Bible points out that wisdom is not something you wait to get until you're older, but something you must gather today: "Wisdom is supreme; therefore get wisdom" (Proverbs 4:7a). God's Word also tells us that wisdom is given to those who seek help: "Pride only breeds quarrels, but wisdom is found in those who take advice" (Proverbs 13:10). You receive wisdom through the godly counsel of seasoned Christians in your life. C. S. Lewis noted, "The next best thing to being wise oneself is to live in a circle of those who are."

Who are three people from your S.H.A.P.E. Training Team you will seek wisdom from as you start to express your Kingdom Purpose?

1. _____

2. _____

3. _____

Ask these individuals to review your Kingdom Purpose so you can make sure it causes you to totally *depend* on God, *display* his love toward others, and *develop* the S.H.A.P.E. he has given you.

If you find yourself unable to say yes to these requirements of a Kingdom Purpose, then go back to Step #1. If you can say yes, great! Enjoy planning your steps toward fulfillment.

Step #5: Plan Your Test-Drive

As you get ready to plan your steps toward further embracing and expressing your unique Kingdom Purpose, let me encourage you to take it for a test-drive. It is during this trip that you start to find "where" you can best express and fulfill your Kingdom Purpose.

Chances are, when you go to buy a car you test-drive it. You want to see if it really fits you and feels right. The same is true as you set out to fully grasp your unique Kingdom Purpose. As you test it, you might realize after five minutes that it's the one for you. However, this process of refinement can take far longer. It took me more than five years of experimenting with various serving opportunities to finally grasp the one thing God has asked me to do on his behalf with the S.H.A.P.E. he has given me. I have discovered in my journey with God that he blesses a moving target.

Another great benefit to test-driving is that it will seal your commitment to do what you were designed to do. I love how Bill Hybels talks about this.

> People who decide to serve in God's mission for as long as he gives them breath ... almost always point back to a specific serving moment that sealed their commitment. "In that moment," they say, "I felt the God of heaven and earth use me, and I discovered that there's nothing

in the world like that. It beats anything else I've ever experienced!" Whether they taught a child how to pray, guided someone toward faith, helped a husband and wife reconcile, served a meal to a homeless person, or produced an audio tape that puts the Christian message in somebody's hand, they knew their lives would never be the same.

Bill goes on to say, "If I had to sum up the key to finding the perfect serving niche, I'd do it in one word: experiment."

As you start to test-drive and experiment with various opportunities—start slow and start small, but most of all just START! Don't sit and wait for the perfect opportunity to come your way ... jump in and test it out as you start serving and blessing others.

I have seen many people reach this point in the process and, with great enthusiasm, decide to start big without taking a test-drive. Some have quit jobs, moved to other states, and sold their homes without much prayer and confirmation. If this describes you, I would ask you to pray each day for the next ninety days, asking God for clarity and confirmation. In addition, make sure your S.H.A.P.E. Training Team agrees 100 percent with your big start. Unless you clearly feel the Lord guiding you, and those championing you agree, start small.

I have seen people who start small finish strong and faithful to what God is asking of them. The Bible says, "'Well done, my good servant!' his master replied. 'Because you have been trustworthy in a very small matter, take charge of ten cities'" (Luke 19:17). Even though John Baker caught a huge vision for Celebrate Recovery, he started small. Only forty-three people attending his first meeting in 1991. Now, fifteen years later, the ministry touches millions of people in several countries. John did what Bill Hybels encourages followers of Christ to do: "Head in the direction of compassion and God will meet you there."

So as you start to plan your Kingdom Purpose test-drive, first focus on making small deposits of compassion into the lives of those around you.

Here are a couple of questions to consider to help you take your test-drive:

- Who are two people you could make a few small deposits of compassion into this week?

   1. _____

2. _____

- What are three to five small steps you could take over the next
  ninety days to start displaying God's love through your Kingdom
  Purpose?

  1. _____

  2. _____

  3. _____

  4. _____

  5. _____

After your test-drive, ask yourself these questions:

- *Did the experience express my Sweet Spot?* If your test-drive requires
  you to serve outside of your Sweet Spot for long periods of time ...
  change cars. If it matches, keep driving and enjoy the journey.
- *Did the experience energize my life?* If your test-drive drains you ...
  change cars! However, if it leaves you with an incredible feeling of
  joy, fulfillment, and excitement, keep driving and serving others.
- *Did the experience express God's love to others?* If so, keep driving! If
  God did not get the glory for your actions, it's time to change cars.

Now, there's one further practical piece of business to attend to—and
that's prioritizing your life to ensure that your Kingdom Purpose test-
drive actually happens.

Statistics show that while millions of people set goals every year, less
than 3 percent ever accomplish them, due in part to the fact that they
don't actually consider how the goals will fit within their schedule. Some
of us are so busy that there is little room left for sleep, much less actual
accomplishment!

What about you? Are you content to blend in with the 97 percent,
spinning your wheels for another year without accomplishing what you
set out to do? We all have the same amount of time to use each week,
168 hours. You can't extend your time, you can't borrow time, you can't

make time, and you can't buy time. You can, however, *prioritize* your time.

Think about the small steps of faith you set above and determine how much time it will take you to complete them. For example, if you figure it will take you five hours over the next month to meet those goals, then you will need to reserve those hours. You may even need to pull them from some other activity that is less important.

Look at your current schedule. What could you stop doing or what could be completed with someone's help so you can focus on the goals you have set with God?

Ask yourself...

- How much time will your small steps of faith take you?
- What days of the week will you commit to?
- What time of day will you shoot for?
- Who will support you?

Putting It All Together

Below you will find space to start building your ninety-day Kingdom Purpose plan—what you will do during your test-drive, when you will do it, and who (from your S.H.A.P.E. Training Team) will help you do it.

Steps of Faith (What?)	Schedule (When?)	Support (Who?)

And for your convenience, I have combined all of this chapter's key exercises in Appendix 2, the S.H.A.P.E. *for* Life Planner on pages 225–227. Even if you wrote responses as you went along, you may want to consolidate your information in that one spot.

Time Out!

We've covered a lot of ground together over the past several pages. If you paused to write responses to the various exercises as you read (which I hope you did!), it's possible you were occasionally stymied by how to answer. That's perfectly normal—these questions about Kingdom Purpose get to the core of who you are, and responding often takes plenty of time and deep thought, not to mention prayer. Please review the material as often as necessary, giving yourself sufficient opportunity to ponder and absorb each point.

Bless Your Church Family

Craig sat across the table from me in my office and said, "Erik, I feel that if I'm going to use to the fullest the gifts and talents God has given me, I need to be in full-time ministry work. I think maybe I should go to Bible college or get a degree in divinity; then I would be ready for ministry." Craig was a very successful corporate executive with a railroad company. He actually loved his job, but felt something was missing.

The next hour, God used me to help Craig see just how special he was and how he could make a significant difference without changing careers. In an email I got later from Craig he wrote, "After meeting with you and working through some exercises, God showed me that I could start doing the things I was designed for now, without quitting my job. That I could use my current job to finance my ministry at church."

Indeed, the best place to start to embrace and express your Kingdom Purpose is at your church. Maybe your idea could become a ministry at your church, and you could become its volunteer leader; just like Craig.

It is so exciting to be able to express your God-given S.H.A.P.E. through your local church. That's how Rick Warren defines the purpose of ministry in *The Purpose Driven® Life* and *The Purpose Driven® Church*.

At Saddleback Church, there are more than 200 ministries that have been started by ordinary people like you, who have embraced their unique S.H.A.P.E. and GRASPed their specific service to God. Because of their faithfulness, these wonderful acts of love and service minister to thousands of people every week.

If you are already part of a church family, share your S.H.A.P.E. and Kingdom Purpose with your pastor and ask about some great places to continue your test-drive. Consider too giving your pastor a copy of this book (Appendix 4 on pages 231–233 is a special note to pastors and church leaders).

If you are not currently part of a local church, find one and make sure it is dedicated to ensuring every member is ministering through their unique God-given S.H.A.P.E.

You Did It!

Congratulations are in order! You have started to discover your special God-given S.H.A.P.E. and define your specific Kingdom Purpose with a short statement.

You have inventoried your life and taken the time to surrender all the "stuff" that has been distracting you and slowing your progress toward fulfilling God's infinitely exciting purpose for your life.

Your thoughts and actions are headed toward reflecting that of a servant. You have begun to assemble a personal team to support you and help you to stay connected to God and committed to fulfilling your Kingdom Purpose. You have started to grasp the dream God has given you for his glory.

Finally, you have drafted a Holy Spirit–guided plan of action to test-drive your purpose, targeted at maximizing your moment on earth for God–all for the greater goal of using your life to bless and serve others.

Now there is only one thing left for you to do–invest your life in helping others discover their unique S.H.A.P.E. and specific purpose for life.

GRABBING HOLD

Reflect on what you have learned. What are a few things you learned about God from this chapter?

Realize what you have been given. Draw a word picture of your unique Sweet Spot below.

Request help from others. What book(s) could you read to help you make the most out of your unique Kingdom Purpose?

Respond in faith. How will your Kingdom Purpose force you to depend on God to fulfill it?

Chapter 11

PASS IT ON

Empowering Those You Love and Lead

Much is required from those to whom much is given,
and much more is required from those to whom much more is given.
Luke 12:48b (NLT)

Mentoring is a lifelong relationship,
in which a mentor helps a protégé
reach her or his God-given potential.
Bob Biehl

Invest your life.

Scott and Kasey, a couple in my Training Group at church, had just returned from their annual meeting with their financial planner. Thanks to some strategic short-term and long-term investments they'd made, they were looking at a solid retirement and the ability to secure their children's educational needs.

It was clear Scott and Kasey had been faithful with the financial blessings God had given them over the years. Now they had the blessing of figuring out how to invest it back into their kids' lives and pay it forward into God's kingdom. They wanted to be certain that what they had would be put to use in people and purposes that would outlive them.

This chapter isn't about finances, but I will apply some basic financial principles to the spiritual realm—investing in God's people and his purposes.

Just like Scott and Kasey's financial plan, your S.H.A.P.E. Investment Plan (how you will pass on what you have learned from this book) will focus on helping the people in your life who you love and lead to be all God created them to be.

Your Circle of Influence

How do you select the best people for your S.H.A.P.E. Investment Plan? I suggest you begin with those with whom you have some level of influence. You don't have to be in an official leadership position to have influence over people. As soon as a person asks for your help, you have an opportunity for influence. Author Tim Elmore explains, "Whatever God has given you that has enabled you to grow and deepen your relationship with him, you can pass on to others." Take the responsibility seriously. Make the most of the opportunity to invest into that individual's life.

As you think about who to invest in, start with the people closest to you. These may include your family, your friends, your coworkers, your classmates, or your small group. You may want to think back to the people you placed on your S.H.A.P.E. Training Team (see chapter nine).

Place your name at the center of the S.H.A.P.E. Investment Circle below. Then add the names of at least ten people, around your name, whose lives you influence in some way. Again, these can be family members, neighbors, friends, work associates, and many others.

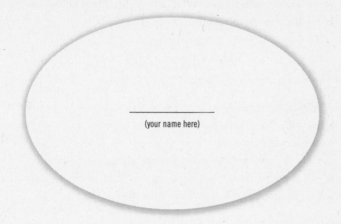

(your name here)

Levels of Influence

Now that you have started to identify the people in your S.H.A.P.E. Investment Circle, it's time to determine the level of influence you have on them. This in turn will help you develop your investment strategy.

Let's consider three levels of influence: Maximum, Moderate, and Minimum.

1. *Maximum Influence:* These are the people in whom your life is most deeply invested. The word *maximum* here does not grant you the right to be invasive or controlling, nor does it give you permission to impose all your ideas, opinions, and beliefs on them. "Maximum" is simply an indicator. For me, this group includes my wife, kids, and close friends. What about you? With whom do you feel you have this level of influence?

2. *Moderate Influence:* These are the people into whose lives you have the ability to speak truth. Usually, you've "earned" this status through a position or past relationship. For me, this group includes some of my neighbors, the people I work with, and the leaders I serve with at Saddleback. What about you? With whom do you have this level of influence?

3. *Minimum Influence:* These are the people with whom you frequently cross paths because of proximity, profession, or personal interests but otherwise don't share a very deep level of relationship. For me, this list includes people who live in my neighborhood and those who I come in contact with at the gym. What about you? With whom do you have this level of influence?

Your S.H.A.P.E. Investment Plan

Just like a well-balanced financial portfolio, a S.H.A.P.E. Investment Plan typically includes both short-term and long-term investments.

As an example, I've outlined my personal S.H.A.P.E. Investment Plan. I hope it sparks some ideas for ways you can make the most out of the relationships God has given you.

▪ ▪ ▪ ▪ ▪

Sample Short-Term Investments: Impacting those over whom I have moderate to minimum influence.

▪ ▪ ▪ ▪ ▪

Investing at Work

Andrea is an outgoing young woman with enormous passion for God and tremendous potential in life. At one time, however, she lacked confidence. Her skills and talents brought her good opportunities at work, but voices from her past were robbing her of the ability to just *be* with God. Something inside told her that her value to God lay in keeping busy. Through a series of relational investments, Andrea finally found that place of true rest with her Creator. Her connection with God became stronger and her S.H.A.P.E. became clearer.

Andrea is one of the wonderful people in whom I have the opportunity to make short-term investments at Saddleback Church. My role there offers me the privilege of investing in the lives of many incredible people who love God and love serving his people. Although the primary focus of what I do is vocational development, God also opens doors for me to help people with spiritual, relational, and emotional growth.

Through these short-term investments, and with God's guidance, I have been able to help people discover their S.H.A.P.E. Our time spent together results in the ability to grasp God's life assignment with greater clarity and confidence.

■ ■ ■ ■ ■

Investing at the Gym

As a sales rep for a life insurance company, Tony's flexible schedule gives him time to work out at lunch most days. I enjoy using my lunch break to play basketball or lift weights. Our paths crossed at our local gym — another place where I find opportunities to make short-term investments.

My routine at the gym has allowed me to build more than a few relational bridges — with men who know God, as well as with those who don't. Tony loves God but says he's too busy with work to serve God in any outside capacity. I encouraged Tony to discover his S.H.A.P.E. and begin to understand what he means to God. Knowing his S.H.A.P.E., I explained, would help him grasp how he could maximize the gifts he has been given. Through God's grace and direction, Tony found his S.H.A.P.E. and is now committed to using it for God's glory.

John, on the other hand, does not yet know God. My short-term investment strategy with John includes prayer and using "God moments" to share godly living with him as our paths cross at the gym. My goal is that John would come to faith in Jesus Christ and begin to discover his

S.H.A.P.E. Although that goal seems distant right now, I still look for ways to plant and water seeds of faith whenever we see each other.

One of my favorite ways to plant seeds with people I meet is to give them a copy of *The Purpose Driven® Life*. This groundbreaking book has struck a chord in millions of lives, with its clear answer to one of life's most perplexing questions: "What on earth am I here for?" It's a question that crosses all faith barriers and the one that both Tony and John are looking to answer.

Who will be listed on your own short-term investment plan? Write down the names of two people from your investment circle who need to discover their God-given S.H.A.P.E. and start embracing their unique purpose for life.

1. _____

2. _____

. . . . .

Sample Long-Term Investments: Impacting those people with whom God has granted me the most influence.

. . . . .

Investing at Home

"You are unbelievably special to God." That's the message I invest in the lives of my wife and kids. My love for them is what motivates me to share this message with them as much as I can, but the methods I use differ. (See Appendix 5: A Note to Couples and Appendix 6: A Note to Parents.)

My wife is a wonderfully gifted woman whose life is fully immersed in her role as a world-class mother, and it's one she would not exchange for anything—not even if it were on sale at Nordstrom! But from time to time she gets a little discouraged. Mothering young children sometimes makes her feel she is not doing enough to make a difference. These are legitimate feelings, but they don't need to pull her away from the value of what she's doing—molding and shaping three young lives. (Not to mention mine!) I want her to realize what D. L. Moody said: "There are many of us that are willing to do great things for the Lord, but few of us are willing to do the little things." So when she struggles with these feelings, I've found that investing love, encouragement, and prayer yield the highest return.

When it comes to my kids' lives, I rely on a combination of prayer, encouragement, and experiences. One of my goals is to pray for my kids every day. I also pray for the wisdom to train them in the way of the Lord. Like all Christian parents, I long for them to follow him with loving and obedient hearts, so I try to do my part in getting them there.

Encouragement comes in daily doses of "verbal vitamins" – the words I speak to my children about God and how special they are to him. We talk about being who God made them to be, not who their friends want them to be. We read the Bible together, looking for verses and chapters that magnify this truth, such as Ephesians 2:10, Jeremiah 29:11, and Philippians 4:13.

I want my kids to have various experiences to discover their spiritual gifts, heart, abilities, and personality. Although they are young, my wife and I can already see unique traits in each one of our kids. All three are competitive, but they seek out opportunities differently. Our oldest enjoys the structure of routine, while our younger two thrive on variety.

At this point in life, our kids' painful experiences are limited to things like falling off their bikes or losing a privilege at home. Still, they are God's masterpieces and God has given each one a special S.H.A.P.E. for serving him. My wife and I love investing our time, love, and resources into their lives. We long for them to experience the joy of knowing and using everything God has given them – and to see each of them make a difference for Christ during their time on earth.

If you have been blessed with the opportunity to be a parent, my challenge to you is to set your long-term investment plan now so God can reap a harvest later. James Dobson writes, "Raising children who have been loaned to us for a brief moment outranks every other responsibility. Besides, living by that priority when kids are small will produce the greatest rewards at maturity."

▪ ▪ ▪ ▪ ▪

Investing at Group

My small group (a.k.a. my Training Group), which I attend with my wife, is another place where I make long-term investments through a combination of cheering, challenging, and counseling.

The five married couples in our group all love God and want to honor him and the S.H.A.P.E. he has given each of us as we navigate our lives with each other. We actually use the concept of S.H.A.P.E. to strengthen our marriages and parenting.

I love cheering for each member of my small group when we are together as well as privately in prayer. I long for each of them to fully embrace their divine design so they can live with the clarity and confidence that only comes from their Creator. Some in the group have done this, while others are still on the path to that goal.

One of the ways I invest in the eternal lives of my small group is to challenge them to embrace and express their S.H.A.P.E. at our group meetings. We are all part of the body of Christ and need each other. For example, Kasey champions prayer requests, Jeff champions our mission projects, and my wife keeps the social calendar current. As you can see, we are better together!

Another way we encourage each other is through prayer. All of us are raising children under the age of thirteen—a task that takes a lot of time and prayer. We all have seen couples literally lose their love for each other by focusing too much on their children. We constantly pray for each other as we all strive to maintain a proper balance.

Another way we invest in each other is by serving one another. For instance, when one couple went away for their anniversary, another couple watched their kids. When my wife had surgery, the other wives brought us meals for a few weeks.

Another way we invest in each other is meeting separately as men and women during the month. The women like to call themselves the "latte ladies," which means they meet at Starbucks for prayer-and-share time. The guys—being guys—have not adopted a group name. We just meet. The objective is to address issues men face—in the home, at work, and in all walks of life. These meetings mean a lot to all of us.

The "counseling" part of this long-term investment strategy occurs naturally as we all do life together. There's nothing formal about it, although there have been times when we have had to intervene in one another's lives. Bottom line, we are motivated to help each other become more mature in our relationship with Jesus.

I can't imagine life without the people in my small group. They all have been instrumental in writing this book. Their reciprocating investments into my life have given me the strength to study and finish what has become a major part of my Kingdom Purpose.

■　■　■　■　■

What about you? Who will be part of your long-term investment plan? Think of two people from your S.H.A.P.E. Investment Circle who could benefit from learning about their God-given S.H.A.P.E. and starting to find their unique purpose for life. Write their names below and ask yourself how you can begin to invest into their lives.

1. _____

2. _____

Now that you know *who* you will be investing in, you need to think about *how* you will get the maximum return on your investments.

Maximizing Your Return on Investment

When I worked in corporate America, we commonly used the term "ROI," or "return on investment." Despite years of throwing that term around, I can't tell you how to get the highest ROI on your financial investments. But I have learned from God how to maximize relational investments for his glory.

Here's a list of ten S.H.A.P.E. Investment Tips to help you get the highest return on the short-term and long-term investments you are committing to make.

1. Accept Your Responsibility

I like to say, "Spot it, you got it." That means if God has shown you someone to help, just help them. Many of us have passed up opportunities to invest in the lives of others, not willing to take the risk. We need to allow God to interrupt us to help others. It stretches us in ways we can't otherwise experience.

The apostle Paul talks about "encouraging, comforting and urging [others] to live lives worthy of God" (1 Thessalonians 2:12). If you love God, then you are responsible to encourage others in their walk with him. Rejoice in this privilege! Seek opportunities and embrace them when God reveals them to you. You'll never regret investing in the life of another person.

2. Ask to Help Them

Once you accept your responsibility to invest in others, invite them to discover their S.H.A.P.E. with you. It's up to you to make that commitment to their growth in Christ. Follow the same method you used in chapter nine when you began building your S.H.A.P.E. Training Team: *pray*, then *pursue*. Take time to pray for each person God has laid on your heart, then pursue them with his guidance. Please don't invite them by email; rather, take the time to personally invite them to journey with you.

3. Affirm Their Decision

When your invitation has been accepted, let them know you are proud of them. Follow the example of the prophet Isaiah by affirming them verbally. The Bible says, "They encourage one another with the words, 'Be strong!'" (Isaiah 41:6, NLT).

4. Authentically Share Your Life with Them

When you meet to begin working this book together, start out your time with prayer and follow that by sharing your personal S.H.A.P.E. discovery experience. Tell them where you were before you read the book. Share what you have learned about yourself, and more significantly, about God. Remember the old saying, "People don't care how much you know until they know how much you care."

5. Appreciate Their Journey

After you have talked about your experiences, listen. Ask them for their stories. Find out why they desire to discover their S.H.A.P.E. Don't rush this step, just let God guide it. If needed, probe gently while remaining tuned in to the Holy Spirit. Just let them know that you appreciate them and are committed to empowering them in their spiritual journey, regardless at what point of the journey they currently find themselves.

6. Admire Their Uniqueness

As you get to know one another, take time to admire their individual S.H.A.P.E. These people may never have taken time to discover who they are. Help them see previously undiscovered facets in the diamonds of their lives. Be a sounding board that affirms and corrects along the way.

In his book, *Mentoring*, Tim Elmore explains the importance of being an encourager to the person you are leading. Elmore uses the biblical example of Barnabas, who saw the potential in Paul despite the intense hatred he had for Christians before his conversion. Barnabas (whose name means "son of encouragement") envisioned Paul's zeal being used *for* God, instead of *against* God and subsequently worked to channel Paul's fierce spirit into becoming a fearless evangelist.

Elmore points out:

> Both Jews and the original disciples alike feared [Paul] and were afraid to let him join them. "But Barnabas took [Saul] and brought him to the apostles" (Acts 9:27). Barnabas was not intimidated by this brash convert, but drew him in and vouched for him. Undoubtedly, he encouraged and taught Saul during those early days and patiently stayed with him, knowing that time and experience would soon temper and mature this gifted young leader.

Elmore asks, "How many Sauls are in the Church today just waiting for a Barnabas?"

7. Apply God's Truth to Every Area of Their Lives

Throughout your journey together, use God's Word to show the way and to shed light on areas that need to be addressed. The Bible says, "You use steel to sharpen steel, and one friend sharpens another" (Proverbs 27:17, MSG). You do this by having courage to ask the tough questions so they can grow from this experience. They should be able to ask themselves if they are going to be known as a cruiser (someone who is apathetic toward life), a consumer (someone who focuses on getting), or a contributor (someone who lives to give).

As you reach chapters seven and eight, on surrender and servanthood, use God's Word to encourage them to set aside things that interfere and distract them from him. Again, be open with your own story and provide them with hope by sharing your struggles and victories. Booker T. Washington said, "Lay hold of something that will help you, and then use it to help somebody else."

8. Assign Them Reasonable and Reachable Goals

When you reach chapter ten, challenge them to go after their Kingdom Dream. If you sense they are a little scared, share your own Kingdom Dream with them. Encourage them to GRASP their Kingdom Purpose, challenging them to get with God so they can discern where he is leading them. When you reach the end of that chapter, make sure they set reachable goals so they will feel like they have some early "wins" as they begin to use what God has given them to bless others.

9. Assist Them Any Way You Can

Let them know you are there for them and are committed to helping them any way you can. If you feel there is an area of their lives that requires help from another source, such as a professional Christian counselor, point them in that direction and let them know you'll stay with them on the way. Do *not* allow yourself to feel pressure to be the one to save this person. God may have given you tremendous positive influence over this person, but it is still God doing the work of salvation. As authors Karen Casey and James Jennings put it so well: "We are the wire, God is the current. Our only power is to let the current pass through us."

10. Analyze Their Progress

This is where your investment *really* begins. Yes, you have put in a lot of time, prayer, and energy up to this point, but only time will reveal if they are willing to grow. As time goes by, you will be able to see if the lessons you have helped them learn truly turn into life application—which should ultimately lead to transformation of mind, heart, and soul.

The Bible says, "And let us consider how we may spur one another on toward love and good deeds" (Hebrews 10:24). Take this verse to heart.

Meet with these people regularly to chart their progress and help them make any necessary course corrections. Consistent meetings will be instrumental in assuring that these brothers or sisters in Christ finish the race with strong faith.

Now that you've read these ten investment tips, look back at tip #2 and decide *who* you will begin investing in.

Invest Now

All of us think we have plenty of time to begin investing into the lives of those God has set aside for us to love and lead. Sadly, this is not always true. Bill Hybels, pastor of Willow Creek Community Church, tells a sobering story about a dad who learned that his three-year-old boy had a brain tumor and that he would have to say goodbye to a son he thought he would be able to love for a lifetime.

Hybels quotes from then-columnist Bob Greene of the *Chicago Tribune*: "Dear Casey, as I lie in bed holding you, I am so painfully aware that you will be with us for only a few more minutes or hours, and my heart breaks when I think of the struggles you have endured in the last eight months. I would give anything to switch places with you.... We will never forget the happiness you brought us. I am the luckiest man in the world to have been your father and friend. I love you madly.... Thanks for being my son. Dad."

"See, that's the thing," Hybels concludes. "You never know how long you have to show love to people in your life. Life is fleeting and fragile."

This moving story clearly shows us that the best time to invest is *now*. You need to plan *now* to pass on what you have learned about God and who he has made each of us to be. Pass it on through short-term and long-term investments in the lives of the people God has put in your path.

The greatest investments you will ever make with your life are those that have an eternal return. Francis of Assisi's wise advice is worth remembering: "Keep a clear eye toward life's end. Do not forget your purpose and destiny as God's creature. What you are in his sight is what you are and nothing more. Remember that when you leave this earth, you can take nothing that you have received ... but only what you have given; a full heart enriched by honest service, love, sacrifice and courage." Plan today to pass on what God has allowed you to learn about your S.H.A.P.E. and Kingdom Purpose.

We've nearly finished our marathon of discovery. Are you tired? About to quit? Don't give up! Find your second wind and get ready to break the tape for God. We're going to learn how to reach your full potential so you can finish well, no matter what.

GRABBING HOLD

Reflect on what you have learned. What did you take away from this chapter about the importance of passing on what you have learned to others?

Realize what you have been given. Write down the names of two people in your everyday walk of life who need to read this book.

Request help from others. Who are two people that have invested in your life over the past year? Call them or send them a note of thanks for the time they have committed to you.

Respond in faith. Write here the name of someone that you currently don't know personally who you would love to meet and learn from. Once you indicate their name, do all you can to connect with them and ask them to share three life lessons with you.

Chapter 12

FULL POTENTIAL

Remaining with the One Who Made You!

Remain in me, and I will remain in you.
No branch can bear fruit by itself;
it must remain in the vine.
Neither can you bear fruit unless you remain in me.
John 15:4

There has never been the slightest doubt
in my mind that the God
who started this great work in you
would keep at it
and bring it to a flourishing finish
on the very day Christ Jesus appears.
Philippians 1:6 (MSG)

Let God complete his work in you.

I remember one other thing from that art class I took in college: Scattered around the room were a handful of unfinished pots. It was obvious something had happened in the middle of the projects that caused students to leave their creations unfinished. The partially shaped pots had collapsed in on themselves and hardened into worthless lumps.

The great news is that God doesn't leave his masterpieces unfinished. The Bible says, "I am sure that God, who began the good work within you, will continue his work until it is finally finished on that day when Christ Jesus comes back again" (Philippians 1:6, NLT). God has every intention of perfecting the work of art he began in your life.

The big difference between you and the clay is that you have to choose to stay on the potter's wheel. Without your cooperation, God will be unable to complete the work he has begun in you. In Romans 12:1, Paul urges us to offer ourselves to God as "living sacrifices." Do you know what the problem is with a living sacrifice? It keeps crawling off the altar!

If you are going to reach your full potential in Christ, you will have to concentrate focused attention on staying close to the Potter and remaining pliable in his hands. Only then can he continue his work of perfecting your S.H.A.P.E.

Thankfully, God gives us a guide to follow – the Bible – and it's full of wisdom and advice to keep us close to him. But we have to build those healthy spiritual habits into our lives. They all require your time, but they promise rewards both now and down the road. I have organized these habits into three categories: Daily, Weekly, and Monthly.

Daily Habits

Surrender to God

The Bible tells us that we are to give ourselves to God as an act of worship: "Therefore, I urge you, brothers, in view of God's mercy, to offer your bodies as living sacrifices, holy and pleasing to God – this is your spiritual act of worship" (Romans 12:1). This act of surrender means allowing him to take full ownership of our life on a daily basis.

No habit will benefit you more than this one. That's because knowing and honoring God with your life is what pleases him most. Use a daily time of surrender to review your list of worries, wounds, wrongs, weaknesses, and wishes to ensure you have given everything to God. In time, your list will get much shorter.

Like a tired runner passing the baton to a fresh teammate, use your time of surrender to pass your burdens to God. Let him carry the weight for you and give you the power to make the most out of each day.

Study God's Word

I don't know who first coined the phrase, "input equals output," but it makes a lot of sense. What enters our minds through our eyes and ears affects what comes out of our mouths.

Every day we have opportunities to read, listen to, and watch things—some good for us, others not so good. Before I became a Christian, I used to listen to Howard Stern's radio program on my way to work. *What was I thinking?* The reality is, I wasn't. Stern's crude humor did nothing positive for my life.

After Christ came into my life, my thinking changed. My desires and habits changed, one thought at a time. God convicted me about my unhealthy habits. Over time, I changed everything I listened to, watched, and read. I wanted God's best for my life. I knew that if I wanted to be in the best spiritual condition for him, I had to fill my mind with only the very best.

The best nourishment for your mind, of course, is God's Word. It is *the* roadmap for life. God's Word is the one thing in life you can trust as *total* truth. It has been—and will always be—powerfully life-changing because God prepared it for us personally. No one wants you to finish life strong more than he does.

God's challenge to Joshua is our challenge today: "Be strong and very courageous. Obey all the laws Moses gave you. Do not turn away from them, and you will be successful in everything you do. Study this Book of the Law continually. Meditate on it day and night so you may be sure to obey all that is written in it. Only then will you succeed. I command you—be strong and courageous! Do not be afraid or discouraged. For the LORD your God is with you wherever you go" (Joshua 1:7–9, NLT).

If you are going to reach your full potential for God, you need to be strong and courageous. But this strength of body and mind only comes from studying and applying God's truth. I love God's choice of words when he said to "meditate" on his truth day and night. As my buddy Lance says, we need to "marinate our minds" with the Word of God.

We need to study God's Word daily, a habit that springs from devotion and not duty. However you do it, don't neglect to study God's love letter to you. Get creative and find the way that best fits your life. Remember, the more you *put in*, the more he will *come out* in your attitude and actions.

Silence Your Heart

Have you ever been in a movie theater and heard someone say, "Quiet, please"? I have. In fact, I'm pretty sure that a time or two they were talking to me! God has had to say "Quiet, please" to me many times. I tend to be a pretty fast-paced, focused individual. I constantly have to remember to slow down and walk *with* God, not miles ahead.

I have a little sign on my computer that reads, "God will speak when you stop." Only when I silence my heart can I seek God with any hope of understanding what he is trying to reveal to me. The Bible says, "Be still in the presence of the LORD, and wait patiently for him to act" (Psalm 37:7a, NLT). The practice of being silent is not easily learned, but it's essential if we are to worship and walk with God effectively. We need to take the time on a daily basis to be still before God.

John Ortberg writes, "Again and again, as we pursue spiritual life, we must do battle with hurry. For many of us the great danger is not that we will renounce our faith. It is that we will become so distracted and rushed and preoccupied that we will settle for a mediocre version of it."

For me, the words *be still* create a mental image of focusing on God in complete peace and relaxation. With distractions, busy schedules, and multiple issues of life all vying for our attention, however, the reality is that being still before God actually requires serious concentration on our part.

Thought it may sound odd, I have learned to practice what I call "flushing my mind" (the act of writing down everything that is swirling in my mind so I can come back to it later) to help me slow down and get to a state of inner silence. We all need to eliminate whatever is wasting our time and energy. I recommend regular "flushing." Whatever it takes for you to learn to slow down and silence yourself before God, *do it*.

Weekly Habits

Set a Day to Honor God

Sunday!! (handwritten)

While preaching to his church congregation in Washington, D.C. on the topic of creating margin, or downtime, in our lives, lead pastor Mark Batterson defined the Sabbath as "a day of rest, a day to recharge our spiritual batteries, a day to refocus on our relationship with God. Jewish rabbis taught that it was a day to let our souls catch up with our bodies. The word *Sabbath* actually means 'to catch one's breath.'"

The Bible says, "By the seventh day God had finished the work he had been doing; so on the seventh day he rested from all his work. And God blessed the seventh day and made it holy, because on it he rested from all the work of creating that he had done" (Genesis 2:2–3).

Author John O'Donohue says, "To be spiritual is to be in rhythm, and that means being devoted to living by the 6:1 rhythm God established at the time of creation."

The fact is, too many of us make God's Sabbath command optional. Only a loving, kind, and gracious God would insist that his children do something so completely valuable and beneficial—simply, *rest!*

God felt so strongly about the Sabbath that he included it in the Ten Commandments:

> Remember the Sabbath day by keeping it holy. Six days you shall labor and do all your work, but the seventh day is a Sabbath to the LORD your God. On it you shall not do any work, neither you, nor your son or daughter, nor your manservant or maidservant, nor your animals, nor the alien within your gates. For in six days the LORD made the heavens and the earth, the sea, and all that is in them, but he rested on the seventh day. Therefore the LORD blessed the Sabbath day and made it holy (Exodus 20:8–11).

Are you having a Sabbath with God—one day a week to rest, setting your focus on him and not on your week's distractions? If not, how will you ever reach your full potential and finish life strong?

Shepherd God's People

Be known as a shepherd for God. Strive each week to maximize the many opportunities he gives you to care for and serve his people. Exercising gentle, caring leadership is a sign of our love for God. It shows our commitment to him.

One day following his resurrection, Jesus asked Simon Peter if he really loved him. Peter's answer mattered so much to Jesus that he actually asked him the question three times, the same number of times Peter had denied him earlier. During the exchange, Jesus said, "If you love me, shepherd my sheep" (my paraphrase, see John 21:15–17). Jesus was not looking for lip service from Peter. He was looking for someone to be a loving servant to his people—he was looking for a shepherd.

When I think of shepherding God's people, I picture someone caring for, loving, supporting, and encouraging others. Do you know anyone who could benefit from a deposit of care, love, support, or encouragement this week?

Make it a goal to shepherd for your Savior each week of your life.

Share God's Love

Before he left earth for heaven, Jesus delivered a message known as the Great Commission in which he told his disciples, "Go and make disciples of all nations, baptizing them in the name of the Father and of the Son and of the Holy Spirit, and teaching them to obey everything I have commanded you. And surely I am with you always, to the very end of the age" (Matthew 28:19–20).

Jesus didn't say, "Go and make disciples of all nations—but only if you have the gift of evangelism." The Great Commission is for all believers. God wants you and I to go verbal with his love to those he has placed around us.

In *The Purpose Driven® Life*, Rick Warren explains, "Jesus calls us not only to come to him, but to go for him." So where can you go for Jesus? Across the street? Across the office? Across the classroom? Across the state? Across the globe? Chances are there are people in your life who either don't know about or have not yet accepted God's love and free gift of eternal life. If you are not sure you know anyone who needs God's love, ask God to show them to you. They are probably closer than you realize.

You may be asking yourself, "What do I say when I go?" Just share your story! Tell them a little about your life before God. Tell them how you found God. Tell them a *lot* about how God has changed your life. All this is your unique story. No one can debate it, because it's *your* story. You are the expert about your story, and no one knows it better than you. God wants you to share it for him.

The Bible says, "Through thick and thin, keep your hearts at attention, in adoration before Christ, your Master. Be ready to speak up and tell anyone who asks why you're living the way you are, and always with the utmost courtesy" (1 Peter 3:15, MSG).

Challenge yourself to share your story with someone at least once a week — and use your S.H.A.P.E. to do it. For instance, if you have the gift of hospitality, use it to create an environment for that person to feel God's love. If you have the gift of mercy, use it to pray for the person. Your passions and personality style can also be very helpful in freeing you up to share your story with clarity and confidence.

You may find this book helpful in sharing God's love. Give it to someone you know who needs God in their life. Everyone wants to find and fulfill their unique purpose in life, so what better tool than a book about that very subject to plant seeds as you share your story with others?

Monthly Habits

Get Away with God

If you want to finish strong for God, it's important to spend quality, uninterrupted time with him. I'm talking about a time of solitude, designed to quiet the noise and the interferences of life for a day or more in order to take inventory of your life. During this time of reflection, make sure God has *all* your life so you are free to receive everything he has for you.

When I recommend a time of solitude, most people react with a look that says, "You must be kidding. And how do you suggest I do that with everything going on in my life?" Dallas Willard offers this advice, "I don't know of any answer to busyness other than solitude."

The Bible says, "Very early in the morning, while it was still dark, Jesus got up, left the house and went off to a solitary place, where he prayed" (Mark 1:35). If Jesus is our ultimate example of how to finish strong, then we should also take from him his example of making solitude something we include in our lives on a regular basis. I suggest a monthly time of getting away with God.

When was the last time you took a personal retreat with God, a time away from all of the sounds of life to just be with your heavenly Father? If you haven't done anything like that recently, plan to do it now. Grab your calendar and mark out at least half a day away with God. Pick a place that helps you disconnect from your routine duties—a retreat center, the park, a hotel, the beach, the mountains. It really doesn't matter what location you choose; what matters is the location of your heart when you get there.

Survey Your Progress

When you're away on your solitude retreat with God, use some of the time to survey your spiritual progress. Ask God to show you how you are doing with your Kingdom Purpose. Review your plan to make sure you are on course. If you find yourself off course, make the adjustments necessary to get back on track. Remember, God is in the fresh-start and course-correction business because he *loves* you!

Also use your retreat time to ask yourself *four key questions* that will help maximize your review. My friend and mentor Tom Paterson calls these "The Four Helpful Questions." Ask God to show you the answers:

1. *What's right in my life?* This is a chance to celebrate what God is doing in you and through you.
2. *What's wrong in my life?* This is a chance for God to reveal some things you need to change in your life.
3. *What's missing from my life?* This is a chance to add something to your life for God.
4. *What's confusing about my life?* This is a chance to clarify some things in your life with God.

Formal getaway or not, make it part of your monthly plan to survey your progress so you can finish strong for God.

Sharpen Your S.H.A.P.E.

The last habit I suggest is regularly sharpening your S.H.A.P.E. for God. The Bible tells us: "If the ax is dull and its edge unsharpened, more strength is needed but skill will bring success" (Ecclesiastes 10:10). My challenge to you is to never stop learning. God deserves your best, so be a continual learner for him.

Rick Warren loves to say, "Leaders are learners." You may not have the title of leader, but if you have the opportunity to influence others at home, work, or in life, you are a leader. That means you not only have an opportunity to lead, but the responsibility as a Christian to lead others according to God's desires.

Make it part of your monthly schedule to sharpen and strengthen your S.H.A.P.E. for God. Dedicate yourself to being the best you can be for his glory.

Take a moment right now to think of two ways you could sharpen your skills this month and then make plans to do them.

See You at the Celebration!

My final message to you is this: *Thank you!*

Thank you for the opportunity to be your companion throughout the pages of this book. Thank you for taking time to discover your God-given S.H.A.P.E.; for striving to find and fulfill your unique Kingdom Purpose; for investing in the lives of others by showing God's love to them. You are indeed a masterpiece!

As we finish, I want to encourage you to go back to your "starting point" (pp. 28–29) and take the short assessment again so you can see just how much God has done in your life since we began this journey together. I also encourage you to take advantage of all the wonderful tools for you online at *www.shapediscovery.com.* This interactive website was designed just for you. And, if you find yourself needing more help or desiring personal one-on-one coaching, please contact me at *coaching@ shapediscovery.com.*

You now have the opportunity to continue what God has started, as you run the next leg of your race with him. May God continue to strengthen you and show you just how special you are. May you live faithful to God and finish fulfilled by him! I will be on the sidelines cheering you on.

And look for me at the finish line, ready to give you the customary, post-race high-five. Until that time, please send me your story at *story@ shapediscovery.com*, so I can hear how God has helped you find and fulfill your unique purpose in life.

GRABBING HOLD

Reflect on what you have learned. What did you learn from this chapter about the importance of rest in your life?

Realize what you have been given. What "habit" are you succeeding at already in your life?

Request help from others. Who will you ask to help hold you accountable to keeping a weekly Sabbath?

Respond in faith. What habit (daily, weekly, monthly) will you commit to adding to your life over the next thirty days?

S.H.A.P.E. *for* LIFE PROFILE

Spiritual Gifts: What I'm gifted to do. (pp. 38–45)

- The spiritual gifts I believe God has given me are:

- I feel I could use these gifts in the following ways to serve others:

Heart: What I have a passion for. (pp. 56–63)

- What drives my life:

- Who I care about most:

- The needs I love to meet in another person's life:

- The cause I feel God wants me to help conquer for him:

- My ultimate dream for God's Kingdom is:

Abilities: What I naturally excel at. (p. 75)

- My top natural abilities are:

Personality: How God has wired me. (pp. 87, 89)

- I tend to *relate* to others by being:

Outgoing	X	Reserved
Self-expressive	X	Self-controlled
Cooperative	X	Competitive

- I tend to *respond* to opportunities that are:

High-risk	X	Low-risk
People	X	Process/Projects
Follow	X	Lead
Teamwork	X	Solo
Routine	X	Variety

Experiences: Where I have been. (pp. 99–105)

- My *positive* experiences include:

- Areas in which I feel I could help another person include:

- My *painful* experiences include:

- These are areas God has helped me through that I feel I could help another person through:

S.H.A.P.E. *for* LIFE PLANNER

Expressing My S.H.A.P.E. for God's Glory

What dream, vison, or message do I feel God nudging me to achieve for him that I couldn't fulfill without him?

My Kingdom Dream (p. 175)

This is how it will cause me to totally *depend* on God ... (p. 176)

This is how it will totally *display* God's love toward others ... (p. 176)

My Serving Sweet Spot (pp. 179–181)

Q1: The spiritual gifts and abilities I believe God has given me to honor him as I step out in faith to fulfill the dream he has given me.

Q2: The people I believe God is calling me to minister to on his behalf.

Q3: The needs I believe God is asking me to meet within the people he is calling me to serve.

Q4: The setting and services I believe my S.H.A.P.E. allows me to offer.

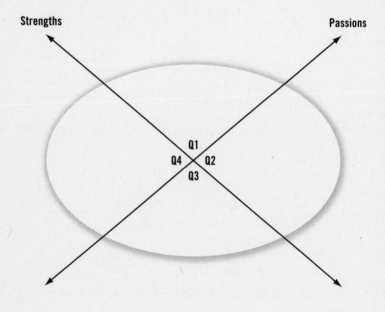

My Kingdom Purpose Statement (p. 182)

God made me …

and when I …

I feel his pleasure.

My Ninety-Day Purpose Plan (p. 187)

Steps of Faith (What?)	Schedule (When?)	Support (Who?)

THE BEST GIFT EVER

As you have been reading in chapter two, God has graced his followers with a variety of spiritual gifts to use to find and fulfill their specific purpose in life. However, there is one special gift that everyone must open and accept *before* they can truly discover the spiritual gifts he has given to them—a gift that truly is "the best gift ever."

This special gift has a special tag on it with your name, a tag that reads: "Your free gift of eternal life." The Bible says, "For it is by grace you have been saved, through faith—and this not from yourselves, it is the gift of God—not by works, so that no one can boast" (Ephesians 2:8–9).

Maybe as you read these words you're realizing you have never opened and accepted God's free gift of eternal life. The truth is, God wants a relationship with you and desires for you to spend eternity with him. But opening the gift and accepting it is your choice.

If you have not accepted this special gift, please do so RIGHT NOW. Don't let another second go by. God knows your heart and will honor your commitment to him. All you need to do is acknowledge what God has done for you, admit your selfishness and sinfulness to him, and ask him into your life. Here's how:

First ...

Acknowledge that God sent his Son, Jesus, for you. The Bible says, "For God so loved the world that he gave his one and only Son, that whoever believes in him shall not perish but have eternal life" (John 3:16).

Then ...

Admit that you, like everyone, are selfish and sinful. The Bible says, "For all have sinned and fall short of the glory of God, and are justified freely by his grace through the redemption that came by Christ Jesus" (Romans 3:23–24). God deeply desires a loving relationship with you. He doesn't want you to try to seek him through different religions, rituals, or rules. He wants you to spend time with him and enjoy his presence in your life.

Next ...

Ask Jesus into your life. The Bible says, "If you confess with your mouth, 'Jesus is Lord,' and believe in your heart that God raised him from the dead, you will be saved" (Romans 10:9). If you have anything to write with, circle *will be saved* and write in the margin, "It's a promise!" The Scripture is very clear: If you confess with your mouth that Jesus is Lord and believe in your heart that God raise him from the dead, then you will live for eternity with God in heaven.

If you desire to open and accept God's gift of eternal life and invite him into a relationship with you, read this prayer to God with all of your heart. As you do, know that I'm agreeing with you:

> *"Dear God, today I fully accept your free gift of eternal life. I confess that I have been living for myself. I recognize that Jesus is the redeemer of my life and I want him to guide me from this point forward. Please help me become the person you made me to be. Please help me to fully understand just how much you love me and how wonderfully you have made me. I want to live for you and fulfill the things you have planned for me. Show me the course to follow so that I can finish faithful to you. In Jesus' name, Amen."*

Congratulations! If you just prayed that prayer and truly meant it in your heart, you now have eternal life with God. I want to encourage you to share your decision with someone in your life. Celebrate your victory point. Now that your destiny is defined by heaven, you can truly start discovering the eternal difference God has planned for you to make on his behalf.

(If you've been reading chapter two, please turn back to page 35.)

A NOTE TO PASTORS AND CHURCH LEADERS

Take a moment and imagine if every person in your church had received a personal invitation from you to express their God-given S.H.A.P.E. through various ministry opportunities that aligned with their unique Kingdom Purpose. WOW! That would certainly bring a smile to God's face: his people serving and strengthening one another just as he designed them to do.

As your heart races with hope and your mind continues to dream of the day when every member in your church is ministering through their S.H.A.P.E., I want to ask three questions:

1. Do *you* truly desire to serve God through your unique S.H.A.P.E.?
2. Do you desire to see *everyone in your church* serving God through their S.H.A.P.E.?
3. Do you know of ministry needs that are going unmet in your church?

If you answered yes to any of these questions, I want to help you learn how to create an empowering culture of ministry in your church!

I love pastors and church leaders. My heart breaks when I hear about those among us who have lost their love for ministry and the joy of serving God and others. Believe me, I've been there more times than I want to admit ... people to help, meetings to attend, emails to write, calls to return, training to develop, the list seems endless.

However, that is not the way God designed it. The Bible clearly tells you and me in Ephesians 4 that we need to be the *administrators* and let the members be the *ministers*; a truth that you MUST embrace if you truly desire to finish the race of ministry faithful and fulfilled.

But how can that happen in the real world of your church? How do you get to the place where every member is involved in ministry? There are three main steps you will need to take to create an empowering culture in your circle of influence.

Step #1

Grasp your ministry by identifying your own unique God-given S.H.A.P.E. and specific Kingdom Purpose—a step I hope this book has allowed you to already begin accomplishing. As you reflect back to chapter eleven—the importance of passing on what God has shown you—I encourage you to start with your staff so they too can express their S.H.A.P.E., then move to your core leadership teams, and finally to the general membership of your church.

Step #2

Give away the rest of your ministry by constantly inviting your members to serve God with you. One way to do this is to dedicate an entire month at your church to the concepts of S.H.A.P.E. and service, culminating with a ministry fair in which you showcase all of your ministries and challenge your members to be not spectators but contributors. To help you discover how to invite your members into ministry, take advantage of the free tips and tools available online at *www.shapediscovery.com.*

Step #3

Grow your members by continually investing in their S.H.A.P.E. This final step to creating a true empowering culture of ministry in your church is all about developing programs that help teach and train your staff, core leaders, and members. Consider starting with a course that focuses on helping your entire church understand what the Bible has to say about S.H.A.P.E. and service.

At Saddleback Church, we use an incredible tool written by Rick Warren entitled: *Class 301, Discovering Your Ministry.* This resource has helped us develop and mobilize thousands of people for ministry effectiveness, and can be adapted for churches of any size. To learn more about this curriculum, visit *www.shapediscovery.com.*

Finally, as you develop your members, readily encourage them to start new ministries within your church that align with their Kingdom Purpose and meet the needs of your people. Ninety-five percent of the ministries at

Saddleback got started by members wanting to make an eternal difference with their lives. We (the staff) just needed to pave the way for them.

No matter where you are in the process right now—even at square one—you can create an empowering culture of ministry in your church that allows you to do your part while everyone else does theirs. Make a covenant with God and watch your church grow.

■ ■ ■ ■ ■

Dear God,

Today I, _____, make a covenant with you to become a change agent for your glory. Please grant me the vision, the passion, and the power to create an empowering culture in my area of influence, ensuring that every member is ministering through their unique S.H.A.P.E. for life.

Signature _____

Date _____

If you would like consulting help as you consider implementing a S.H.A.P.E. discovery process within your church, please contact me at *consulting@shapediscovery.com.*

God bless,
Erik

A NOTE TO COUPLES

Wives, understand and support your husbands by submitting
to them in ways that honor the Master.
Husbands, go all out in love for your wives.
Don't take advantage of them.
Colossians 3:18–19 (MSG)

It starts with acceptance.

During the first few years of my marriage I had to learn to cherish my wife rather than try to change her. God calls me to love her like nothing else, but I have to admit it was a steep learning curve for me. One of the things that dramatically helped me to understand and support her was discovering her unique S.H.A.P.E. You know what I found out? She was nothing like me! The fact was, she was the opposite of me. Her gifts were different than mine. Her heart beat for topics that I had little interest in. Her abilities and mine seldom matched. A few of her personality styles were the opposite of mine. And our experiences were totally different. Yet no matter how different we were, God still called me to accept her with my actions and affirm her with my words.

Today, we both are committed to accepting and appreciating each other so we help each other fulfill our unique purpose in life. Specifically, we focus on three things:

Cherishing Each Other's S.H.A.P.E.

The first thing we had to learn about each other was our uniqueness. We took tests, attended classes, talked to other couples, and spent a lot of time just learning about things we had in common and things we didn't. These investments have helped us understand each other better than we ever have before.

Championing Each Other's Kingdom Purpose

Once we learned how God made each of us unique, we started to discover our individual purposes for life. My wife feels that one of her major contributions is being a world-class mother, which she is. She uses her S.H.A.P.E. to cultivate our kids in so many great ways. She also has a few other kingdom passions that she expresses from time to time. I try to champion all she dreams of doing for God's glory. Conversely, my wife constantly champions my purpose in life, which is to empower every believer in the world with proven tools so they can find and fulfill their unique purpose in life by embracing and expressing their God-given S.H.A.P.E.

Cheering for Each Other Constantly

Besides cheering for our kids, we love cheering for each other. We want to be each other's biggest fans with our words, with our actions, and most importantly with our prayers. We pray that God would use both of us individually and collectively to make a kingdom difference for his glory.

If you are married, I strongly encourage you to not only discover your S.H.A.P.E. and purpose for life, but give a copy of this book to your spouse to do the same. Then the two of you can cherish, champion, and cheer for each other and make a significant kingdom difference together!

A NOTE TO PARENTS

Train a child in the way he should go, and when he is old he will not turn from it.
Proverbs 22:6

You can do it!

By now I hope you have discovered your God-given S.H.A.P.E. and have started to define your specific purpose in life. But what about your kids? As parents of three children, my wife and I desire to do all we can to help train them in the way they were designed by God to go. We are constantly thinking about ways to cultivate our kids' uniqueness, from helping them discover their special gifts to understanding how God can use their experiences to serve others and share his love.

The truth is, children come pre-wired but they don't come with an owner's manual. I wish they did, but then we wouldn't need to depend on God to help us. As parents, we have the opportunity to help them discover their uniqueness so they too can find and fulfill their purpose in life as they get older. What a great privilege! But what a great challenge. In fact, a survey we conducted at Saddleback Church indicated that a majority of parents would love some help in this all-important training. In that vein, here are three keys—the ABCs—to helping your kids reach their God-given potential:

Accept Your Responsibility

As a parent, YOU are responsible for training your child. No one else can do it for you. You can seek help from your church and extended family, of course, but ultimately, God holds you accountable. Don't worry, you can do it ... but first you must *accept* the responsibility and ask God for wisdom and strength daily, if not hourly.

As you accept your responsibility, remember God calls us to train our kids in THE way they should go. Not the way *we* want them to go. Far too often, parents (myself included) want their kids to go the way the parents decide without ever taking the time to discover the way God designed them.

From one parent to another, please accept your responsibility so your kids will always know that YOU are their biggest champion and cheerleader!

Become Who God Shaped You to Be First

Do you realize your kids are watching and listening to you? They are—more than you know. The fact is, we can't pass on what we don't possess ourselves. We can try, but it won't last. I like to tell parents, "It's not what you say that matters most, it's what your kids see." As you commit to becoming who God shaped you to be and fulfilling your unique purpose in life, enjoy the great opportunity to pass on these great truths of God to your kids.

Cultivate Their S.H.A.P.E.

After you have accepted your responsibility to train your children and have committed to becoming who God shaped you to be, then you can move to the final step ... cultivating *their* unique S.H.A.P.E.

I have seen the concepts of S.H.A.P.E. work with kids as young as seven years old. Children understand more than you think they do. It continues to amaze me how much my own kids comprehend stuff that I thought was "over their heads."

Specifically, a great way to cultivate your kids' uniqueness is to apply to them the ten S.H.A.P.E. Investment Tips from chapter 11 (see pp. 201–204). These simple guidelines will provide a great path to follow as you train your children in the way they should go.

Coming spring 2008 from ZonderKidz!

Only You Can Be You: Finding Your Serving Sweet Spot
BY ERIK REES

Written especially for children ages 8–12

ISBN: 0-310-71409-5

GRABBING HOLD TOGETHER

Group Discussion Guide

The topics covered in *S.H.A.P.E.* are ideal to discuss with other people interested in finding and fulfilling their Kingdom Purpose, whether informally or as part of a churchwide study. If you would like, use the following guide to direct your time together. Each of the thirteen sessions, one for the introduction ("A Message from the Author") and one for each book chapter, is organized into four key sections:

1. **Looking At:** Considering a Bible passage together.
2. **Looking In:** Discussing your personal observations, how you expect God to change *you* through this study.
3. **Looking Around:** Discussing how God can work through the group, his body, through this study.
4. **Looking Up:** Praying together as a group that God will produce direction, spiritual maturity, and fruit through this study.

A Message from the Author

Looking At

Discuss the following passage as a group and the process it outlines for discovering who we are:

> Make a careful exploration of who you are and the work you have been given, and then sink yourself into that. Don't be impressed with yourself. Don't compare yourself with others. Each of you must take responsibility for doing the creative best you can with your own life (Galatians 6:4–5, MSG).

Looking In

Share your responses with the group:

- What is one thing that you desire for God to do *in you* during this study?
- What is one thing that you desire for God to do *through you* by the end of this study?

Looking Around

Discuss the following question as a group:

- What is one thing that you desire for God to do in *your group* during this study?

Looking Up

Pair up with someone in your group and pray for each other's answers to the above questions.

Chapter 1: Masterpiece

Looking At

Discuss the following verse as a group and how it relates to your individual lives:

For we are God's masterpiece. He has created us anew in Christ Jesus, so that we can do the good things he planned for us long ago (Ephesians 2:10, NLT).

Looking In

Share your responses with the group:

- How does it make you feel knowing that God sees you as a masterpiece? Then share any specific events from your past that have either helped you feel this way or hindered you from seeing yourself as God's masterpiece.
- What would be two "good works" that you think God wants to achieve through you?
- Take the personal inventory on pages 28–29 and share what category you currently fall in and why.

Looking Around

Discuss the following questions as a group:

- The author says God has given each of us a unique S.H.A.P.E. for life and desires for us to use it to make a difference for him on earth. Describe with the group how this statement should affect the body of Christ.
- Do you know your unique Kingdom Purpose for life? If so, share it with the group. If not, ask someone in the group to pray for God to reveal it to you as you journey through this material with each other.

Looking Up

Use your group prayer time to celebrate each other's uniqueness and contribution to the group.

Chapter 2: Spiritual Gifts

Looking At

Discuss the following verse as a group and what God is asking of us as his followers:

Each one should use whatever gift he has received to serve others, faithfully administering God's grace in its various forms (1 Peter 4:10).

Looking In

Share your responses with the group:

- What thought, word, or idea comes to mind when you think about being gifted for greatness?
- What gifts do you believe God has specifically given you? Why?
- How do you think you can use your gifts to "serve" others?

Looking Around

Discuss the following questions as a group:

- How can your specific gifts help strengthen your group and help serve one another?

- The author talks about four common traps that can hinder us from using our gifts the way God intended them to be used. To what trap are you most susceptible? How can your group help you to avoid this trap?

Looking Up

Pair up with someone in the group and pray for each other to be accountable not only to avoiding Satan's traps but to using the spiritual gifts God has given each of you.

Chapter 3: Heart

Looking At

Discuss the following passage as a group and the position our heart must be in to be rewarded by God:

> Whatever you do, work at it with all your heart, as working for the Lord, not for men, since you know that you will receive an inheritance from the Lord as a reward. It is the Lord Christ you are serving (Colossians 3:23–24).

Looking In

Share your responses with the group:

- What things in life cause your heart to race for God? How can you use these things to display God's love?
- What specific group of people does your heart beat for? Why? How have you used your gifts to serve this group of people?

Looking Around

Discuss the following questions as a group:

- What needs do you love meeting on behalf of God? Who else in your group shares the same passion? Talk about ways you all can use your combined passion to serve God together.
- What cause do you feel drawn to help conquer? Does it match with Kay's or Millard's or someone in your group?

Looking Up

Divide your group into two small groups for prayer time. Share a God-centered dream with each other and then pray over these dreams together.

Chapter 4: Abilities

Looking At

Discuss the following verse as a group and how it relates to your individual lives as well as to the group's potential strength:

> God has given each of us the ability to do certain things well (Romans 12:6a, NLT).

Looking In

Share your responses with the group:

- Describe a time in your life that you had to do something that left you feeling exhausted because it simply was not something you were good at.
- What are three things you could "live without" doing?

Looking Around

Discuss the following questions as a group:

- What are three things you just love doing? Share these activities with the group and how they could be used to display God's love to those around you.
- Does anyone in your group excel at the same things? If so, talk about how you could serve others together.
- How could everyone's natural abilities strengthen your small group?

Looking Up

Use your prayer time to celebrate the natural abilities God has given to each member of the group and how the group benefits when each person is using their strengths.

Chapter 5: Personality

Looking At

Discuss the following passage as a group and how it shows different personalities:

> As Jesus and his disciples were on their way, he came to a village where a woman named Martha opened her home to him. She had a sister called Mary, who sat at the Lord's feet listening to what he said. But Martha was distracted by all the preparations that had to be made. She came to him and asked, "Lord, don't you care that my sister has left me to do the work by myself? Tell her to help me!"
>
> "Martha, Martha," the Lord answered, "you are worried and upset about many things, but only one thing is needed. Mary has chosen what is better, and it will not be taken away from her" (Luke 10:38–42).

Looking In

Share your responses with the group:

- Describe your personality style to the group.
- Share a time in your life that you were asked to step outside your personality comfort zone and how it made you feel.

Looking Around

Discuss the following questions as a group:

- What are a few ways your group's personality styles can strengthen the group as a whole?
- How can you use your collective personality styles to serve someone in need around you within the next thirty days?

Looking Up

Use your prayer time to pray for the person/family/people you indicated above that your group will try to find opportunity to serve in the next thirty days.

Chapter 6: Experiences

Looking At

Discuss the following passage as a group and how it relates to our experiences:

> Praise be to the God and Father of our Lord Jesus Christ, the Father of compassion and the God of all comfort, who comforts us in all our troubles, so that we can comfort those in any trouble with the comfort we ourselves have received from God (2 Corinthians 1:3–4).

Looking In

Share your responses with the group:

- Describe for the group one positive and one painful portrait from your "hallway of life."
- Share with the group how these two portraits can be used to display God's love to others around you.

Looking Around

Discuss the following questions as a group:

- Share a positive experience you have had in this or another group and how it impacted the group.
- Share with each other a painful experience you have had in this or another group and how it impacted the group.

Looking Up

For your prayer time, split up into two smaller groups and ask the others in your sub-group to pray for a painful experience in your life that still has a grip on you.

Chapter 7: Letting Go

Looking At

Discuss the following passage as a group, specifically what it asks us to let go of in our lives:

> Therefore, since we are surrounded by such a huge crowd of witnesses to the life of faith, let us strip off every weight that slows us down, especially the sin that so easily hinders our progress. And let us run with endurance the race that God has set before us. We do this by keeping our eyes on Jesus, on whom our faith depends from start to finish (Hebrews 12:1–2a, NLT).

Looking In

Share your responses with the group:

- What currently is slowing you down or distracting you from being all God made you to be?
- Have you fully surrendered everything (worries, wounds, wrongs, weaknesses, wishes) to God? If so, share your surrender moment with the group. If not, consider using your group time to surrender today.

Looking Around

Discuss the following questions as a group:

- Are there any issues in your group that are weighing it down or distracting it from being all God desires for it?
- What might it mean/look like to surrender corporately—as a group, as a church?

Looking Up

During your prayer time, pair up with someone else in the group and read the following verses aloud together. Then confess anything that God brings to the surface.

> Search me, O God, and know my heart; test me and know my thoughts. Point out anything in me that offends you, and lead me along the path of everlasting life (Psalm 139:23–24, NLT).

Chapter 8: Other-Centered

Looking At

Discuss the following passage as a group and how it should impact our daily life:

> Whoever wants to become great among you must be your servant, and whoever wants to be first must be your slave—just as the Son of Man did not come to be served, but to serve, and to give his life as a ransom for many (Matthew 20:26–28).

Looking In

Share your responses with the group:

- Describe a time that you modeled the behavior of the Good Samaritan and how it made you feel.
- When asked to use your resouces to meet the needs of others, what typically is your first response and why?

Looking Around

Discuss the following questions as a group:

- What obstacles, if any, have kept your group from together serving others outside the group?
- What is more important to God ... stewardship of your strengths or having a servant heart? Why? Use Scripture to back up your thoughts.

Looking Up

Use your prayer time to celebrate the one person (or two) in your group who best expresses and models an "other-centered" lifestyle.

Chapter 9: Better Together

Looking At

Discuss the following passage as a group, and share how your group has modeled these characteristics of love toward each other:

> Love is patient, love is kind. It does not envy, it does not boast, it is not proud. It is not rude, it is not self-seeking, it is not easily angered, it keeps no record of wrongs. Love does not delight in evil but rejoices with the truth. It always protects, always trusts, always hopes, always perseveres (1 Corinthians 13:4–7).

Looking In

Share your responses with the group:

- Point to a time in your life that you told someone you were doing "fine" but you really weren't. What kept you from sharing your true feelings?
- Share a time when someone spoke truth to you and you did or didn't have "ears to hear" what was being shared. How did that experience affect your life?

Looking Around

Discuss the following questions as a group:

- The author stated, "When competition decreases – community increases." Is there any competition among your group members? If so, talk about it and how it might keep your group from developing true community with each other.
- Share with each other who you invited to be part of your personal Board of Advisors and how they will strengthen your life.

Looking Up

During your prayer time, split into two smaller groups. Ask group members to pray for the people you desire to pursue and place on your S.H.A.P.E. Training Team.

Chapter 10: Kingdom Purpose

Looking At

Discuss the following passage as a group, specifically how trust plays a vital role in our ability to find and fulfill our Kingdom Purpose:

> We are confident of all this because of our great trust in God through Christ. It is not that we think we can do anything of lasting value by ourselves. Our only power and success come from God (2 Corinthians 3:4–5, NLT).

Looking In

Share your responses with the group:

- How does dreaming for God's kingdom make you feel? Why?
- Share a detailed word portrait of your Kingdom Dream.
- Describe your Serving Sweet Spot to the group.
- Share your draft Kingdom Purpose Statement with each other.
- How do you intend to "test-drive" your Kingdom Purpose over the next ninety days?

Looking Around

Discuss the following questions as a group:

- If you have not been able to GRASP your Kingdom Purpose as of yet, use your group time to help each other do so. Start with the oldest member in your group and end with the youngest. Ask God to give you all breakthrough thinking. This could take a few group meetings, but that is okay.
- Share with one another any fears you may have about finding and fulfilling your Kingdom Purpose.

Looking Up

Focus your prayer time on asking God to give those members of the group who have not yet drafted a Kingdom Purpose Statement the clarity and confidence to do so.

Chapter 11: Pass It On

Looking At

Discuss the following passage as a group, specifically what God is clearly asking of each of us as his followers:

> Much is required from those to whom much is given, and much more is required from those to whom much more is given (Luke 12:48b, NLT).

Looking In

Share your responses with the group:

- Describe a time when someone invested into your life and how it made you feel.
- Describe a time when you invested into someone else's life and how it made you feel.
- Share the name of one person you would like to start investing in.

Looking Around

Discuss the following questions as a group:

- Is there someone outside of your group whom you could invite to join your group so you could collectively invest into that person's life?
- How has your group coached each other, cheered for each other, and helped counsel each other during your time together?

Looking Up

During your prayer time, pray for the person on your right, particularly their desire to invest into the life they mentioned earlier. Pray that God would give this fellow group member boldness and that he would prepare the individual's heart to accept the group member's invitation.

Chapter 12: Full Potential

Looking At

Discuss the following passage as a group and what it means to each person.

> And I am sure that God, who began the good work within you, will continue his work until it is finally finished on that day when Christ Jesus comes back again (Philippians 1:6, NLT).

Looking In

Share your responses with the group:

- How has God kept you "pliable" in life?
- Would you say "silencing" your heart is easy or hard? Explain your answer.
- Retake the inventory on pages 28–29 and note how God has brought more clarity to your life during this study. Share your insights with the group.

Looking Around

Discuss the following questions as a group:

- How easy or difficult is it for each group member to fulfill God's command to have a weekly Sabbath? Feel free to offer any tips you have found helpful in achieving a time apart with God.
- Share your "Kingdom Purpose Statement" if you weren't able to define it in chapter ten. Also share how your "test-drive" is going.
- How can we help sharpen each other's S.H.A.P.E.?

Looking Up

Conclude this study in celebratory praise to God for his grace and goodness demonstrated in your group. Thank him for all he has done in each person separately and through the group collectively.

SOURCES

A Message from the Author

11: Rick Warren, *The Purpose Driven® Life*. Grand Rapids, Mich.: Zondervan, 2002, 232.

Chapter 1: Masterpiece

19: Rick Warren, *The Purpose Driven® Life*. Grand Rapids, Mich.: Zondervan, 2002, 241.

20: Max Lucado, *You Are Special*. Nashville: Thomas Nelson, 1997.

20–21: Tom Paterson. From an email to the author. Used by permission.

21: Max Lucado, *Cure for the Common Life*. *www.maxlucado.com*, *Cure for the Common Life* webinar video transcript.

24–25: Rick Warren, *The Purpose Driven® Church*. Grand Rapids, Mich.: Zondervan, 1995, 369–70.

26–27: Description of Henri Matisse's *The Dance* and Claude Monet's *Water Lilies* adapted from the State Hermitage Museum's website, http://www.hermitagemuseum.org/html_En/08/hm88_0_2_70_1.html, http://www.hermitagemuseum.org/html_En/04/b2003/hm4_1_14.html. The State Hermitage Museum, St. Petersburg, Russia.

27: Description of Vincent Van Gogh's *The Starry Night* adapted from WebMuseum at http://www.ibiblio.org/wm/paint/auth/gogh/starry-night.

Chapter 2: Spiritual Gifts

32: Leslie B. Flynn, *19 Gifts of the Spirit*. Colorado Springs: Cook Communications, 1974, 1994, 17–18.

34: Ibid., 27.

34: Os Guinness, *The Call: Finding and Fulfilling the Central Purpose of Your Life*. Nashville: W Publishing, 2003, 45.

36: Rick Warren, *The Purpose Driven® Life*, 251.

46: Helen Keller. Quoted in Susan Miller, *True Woman: The Beauty and Strength of a Godly Woman*. Wheaton, Ill.: Crossway, 1997, 112.

46–47: Arthur F. Miller Jr., *Why You Can't Be Anything You Want to Be*. Grand Rapids, Mich.: Zondervan, 1999, 237, 238.

49: Warren, *The Purpose Driven® Life*, 255.

50: Erwin Raphael McManus, *Seizing Your Divine Moment*. Nashville: Thomas Nelson, 2002, 76–77.

Chapter 3: Heart

55–56: Tom Paterson, *Living the Life You Were Meant to Live*. Nashville: Thomas Nelson, 1998, 155.

56: Rick Warren, *The Purpose Driven® Life*, 238.

58: Dwight L. Moody anecdote. *Today in the Word*, February 1, 1997, 6.

62–63: John Eldredge, *Wild at Heart – Field Manual*. Nashville: Thomas Nelson, 2001, 248.

Chapter 4: Abilities

69: Rick Warren, *The Purpose Driven® Life*, 244.

69: Robin Chaddock, *Discovering Your Divine Assignment*. Eugene, Ore.: Harvest House, 2005, 78.

70–71: Max Lucado, *Shaped by God*. Wheaton, Ill.: Tyndale, 1985, 3–4.

72: Arthur F. Miller Jr., *Why You Can't Be Anything You Want to Be*, 111.

72–73: Andrew Murray, *Absolute Surrender*. Minneapolis: Bethany House, 1985, 78.

77: Pat Williams, Jay Strack, and Jim Denney, *The Three Success Secrets of Shamgar*. Deerfield Beach, Fla.: Faith Communications, 1973, 4, 26.

78: C. S. Lewis, *The Weight of Glory*. New York: HarperCollins, 1949, 26.

Chapter 5: Personality

82: Gary Smalley and John Trent, *The Two Sides of Love*. Colorado Springs: Focus on the Family Publishing, 1999.

82: Florence Littauer, *Personality Plus: How to Understand Others by Understanding Yourself* (revised, expanded edition). Grand Rapids, Mich.: Revell, 1992, 14–15.

82–83: Arthur F. Miller Jr., *Why You Can't Be Anything You Want to Be*, 190.

83: Rick Warren, *The Purpose Driven® Life*, 245.

84: Jane A. G. Kise, David Stark, and Sandra Krebs Hirsh, *LifeKeys: Discovering Who You Are, Why You're Here, What You Do Best*. Minneapolis: Bethany House, 1996, 126.

84: Miller, *Why You Can't Be Anything You Want to Be*, 11.

92: Bob Briner, *Roaring Lambs: A Gentle Plan to Radically Change Your World.* Grand Rapids, Mich.: Zondervan, 1993, 18.

92: Kise, Stark, and Hirsh, *LifeKeys*, 156.

Chapter 6: Experiences

98: Arthur F. Miller Jr., *The Truth about You.* Old Tappan, N.J.: Fleming H. Revell, 1977, 22.

106: Max Lucado, *Shaped by God*, 50–51.

110: Ibid., 173.

Chapter 7: Letting Go

116: Andrew Murray, *Absolute Surrender*, 80.

117: Brad Johnson. Quoted from a message at Saddleback Church, July 24, 2005.

118: David G. Benner, *Surrender to Love.* Downers Grove, Ill.: InterVarsity Press, 2003, 81, 82.

118–19: Max Lucado, *Shaped by God*, 112.

119–20: Rick Warren, *The Purpose Driven® Life*, 83–84.

125: John Ortberg, *The Life You've Always Wanted.* Grand Rapids, Mich.: Zondervan, 1997, 122.

127: Brad Johnson. Quoted from a message at Saddleback Church, July 24, 2005.

128: Bruce Wilkinson, *The Dream Giver.* Sisters, Ore.: Multnomah, 2003, 75.

129: Warren, *The Purpose Driven® Life*, 80–81.

Chapter 8: Other-Centered

134–35: Ashley Smith story. Ashley Smith with Stacy Mattingly, *Unlikely Angel.* Grand Rapids, Mich.: Zondervan, 2005.

140: Andrew Murray, *Humility.* Minneapolis: Bethany House, 1973, preface.

Chapter 9: Better Together

153: John Ortberg, *The Life You've Always Wanted*, 43.

Chapter 10: Kingdom Purpose

171: Bruce Wilkinson, *The Dream Giver*, 6.

172: Jim Collins, *Good to Great.* New York: HarperCollins, 2001, 232–34.

172–73: Chip Ingram, *Holy Ambition.* Chicago: Moody Press, 2002, 116–17.

173: Rick Warren, *The Purpose Driven® Life*, 292–93.

184–85: Bill Hybels, *The Volunteer Revolution.* Grand Rapids, Mich.: Zondervan, 2004, 15, 67.

Chapter 11: Pass It On

194: Tim Elmore, *Mentoring: How to Invest Your Life in Others.* Atlanta: EQUP, 1998, 18.

199: James Dobson, *Bringing Up Boys.* Wheaton, Ill.: Tyndale, 2001, 247.

203: Elmore, *Mentoring*, 21–22.

204: Karen Casey and James Jennings, *In God's Care: Daily Meditations on Spirituality in Recovery.* Deerfield Beach, Fla.: Hazelden, 1991, 5.

205: Bill Hybels, "Love of Another Kind" sermon series.

Chapter 12: Full Potential

212: John Ortberg, *The Life You've Always Wanted*, 82.

213: Mark Batterson, National Community Church, *www.theaterchurch.com*, posted January 14, 2003.

213: John O'Donohue, *Anam Cara: A Book of Celtic Wisdom.* New York: HarperCollins, 1998, 85.

214: Rick Warren, *The Purpose Driven® Life*, 282.

215: Dallas Willard. Quoted in an online devotional by Mark Batterson, *www.theaterchurch.com*, posted January 14, 2003.

216: Tom Paterson, *Living the Life You Were Meant to Live*, 80.

We want to hear from you. Please send your comments about this book to us in care of zreview@zondervan.com. Thank you.

GRAND RAPIDS, MICHIGAN 49530 USA

ZONDERVAN.COM/
AUTHOR**TRACKER**